P9-DNO-339

At ✳ Issue

What Causes Addiction?

Mercedes Muñoz, *Book Editor*

Bruce Glassman, *Vice President*
Bonnie Szumski, *Publisher*
Helen Cothran, *Managing Editor*

GREENHAVEN PRESS
An imprint of Thomson Gale, a part of The Thomson Corporation

THOMSON
———✳———
GALE

Detroit • New York • San Francisco • San Diego • New Haven, Conn.
Waterville, Maine • London • Munich

For more information, contact
Greenhaven Press
27500 Drake Rd.
Farmington Hills, MI 48331-3535
Or you can visit our Internet site at http://www.gale.com

LIBRARY OF CONGRESS CATALOGING-IN-PUBLICATION DATA
What causes addiction? / Mercedes Muñoz, book editor.
p. cm. — (At issue)
Includes bibliographical references and index.
ISBN 0-7377-2755-1 (lib. : alk. paper) —
ISBN 0-7377-2756-X (pbk. : alk. paper)
1. Drug abuse. I. Muñoz, Mercedes. II. At issue (San Diego, Calif.)
HV5801.W417 2005
616.86—dc22   2004060564

Printed in the United States of America

Contents

Introduction

Out of all the people who experiment with illicit drugs or alcohol, relatively few become addicts. While experts agree on a variety of reasons for why people experiment with addictive substances (curiosity, recreation, self-medication), there is little agreement on what causes people to progress from use of a substance to addiction. Many experts now agree that addiction is a brain pathology, but understanding why some brains become addicted and others do not is likely to be debated for some time to come. Indeed, addiction research has been hampered by numerous obstacles, from a lack of appropriate technology to study the brain to federal laws regulating drugs.

For decades studies on the effects of addictive substances were limited by technology. While scientists have been scanning the human brain since 1918, it was only in the 1970s, with the development of positron-emission tomography (PET) and magnetic resonance imaging (MRI), that researchers could safely and repeatedly scan the brain without risking harm to the patient. As a result, scientists are now able to map the areas of the brain that different drugs affect and better understand the consequences of drug and alcohol abuse. For example, using these technologies, researchers have discovered that cocaine and amphetamines raise the amount of dopamine in the brain, producing an increased sense of pleasure. Scientists also have learned that the hallucinations caused by LSD are a result of the drug's effect on Type 2 serotonin receptors. In addition, researchers at the University of California, San Diego, have found that teenagers who consume an average of two drinks a day for two years risk losing 10 percent of their memories.

Although improved brain scanning techniques have increased understanding of the effects of drugs, government regulations still make it difficult for researchers to examine the process of addiction in humans. All drugs are classified into five levels (Schedules) of control. Schedule V drugs, which may be purchased over the counter at a pharmacy, include cough and cold medicines. Schedule IV drugs are considered to have slightly more potential for abuse and require a doctor's prescription.

Schedule III drugs have accepted medical uses but are considered to be addictive. Drugs under Schedule II are considered to have a very high potential of abuse, and there are strict regulations for the circumstances under which doctors may prescribe them. Schedule II drugs include cocaine, morphine, and phencyclidine (PCP). Like Schedule II drugs, Schedule I drugs are considered to have a very high potential of abuse, but unlike Schedule II substances, these drugs may not be prescribed by a physician as they have no accepted medical use. Some examples of Schedule I drugs are marijuana, heroin, and MDMA (ecstasy).

The restrictions on Schedule I and Schedule II drugs mean that the majority of studies on the addictiveness of heroin, cocaine, marijuana, and even alcohol cannot be performed on humans. Instead, these drugs are usually tested on rats. The results of these studies are often questioned. Critics argue that studies on how certain drugs affect rats say very little about how humans in real-life situations would react to the same substances. Jacob Sullum, author of *Saying Yes*, writes,

> Such studies . . . tell us little about animal behavior in more naturalistic settings, let alone human behavior in the real world. Traumatized by the implantation of the catheter, the animals are kept in isolated cages with little to stimulate them or soothe them except the drug running through the tube. . . . When [humans] are bored, lonely, and in pain, they are more apt to use drugs heavily. And since humans can look to the future, the prospects they perceive for improving their situation also affect their drug use.

To be sure, federal drug laws and technological limitations have hampered researchers' investigations into the nature of addiction. Still, experts have devised numerous theories explaining why some drug users become addicted while others do not. Discovering what causes addiction could have an enormous impact on those struggling with drug abuse and their families.

1

Addiction Is a Brain Disease

Ernest Drucker

Ernest Drucker is the director of the Division of Public Health and Policy Research at Montefiore Medical Center and a professor at Albert Einstein College of Medicine, both in New York City. He researches AIDS, drug use, and drug policy.

Drug use changes the body's neurotransmission, gradually leading to addiction. Drug users go through several stages in their development of addiction. Tolerance is developed with repeated drug use. Withdrawal occurs when drug use ends, and craving occurs when the body needs the drug to feel normal. Unfortunately, while the majority in the medical establishment recognize addiction as a brain disease, American society persists in viewing it as a moral and legal problem.

Although the word *addiction* does not appear in medical usage until the mid 19th century, by that time, millions of Americans and Europeans were habitual users of [prescription or over-the-counter drugs containing some combination of opiates, cocaine, and alcohol], and many were considered dependent on them. Although this group represented only a minority of all those who used these drugs, even of those who used them often, "drug addicts" (generally a pejorative term) came to occupy the most prominent place in the public debate about drugs. It was clear that dependent individuals not only used a given drug to relieve the symptoms of illness and for the

Ernest Drucker, "From Morphine to Methadone: Maintenance Drugs in the Treatment of Opiate Addiction," *Harm Reduction: National and International Perspectives*, edited by James A. Inciardi and Lana D. Harrison. Thousand Oaks, CA: Sage Publications, Inc., 2000. Copyright © 2000 by Sage Publications, Inc. All rights reserved. Reproduced by permission.

beneficial effects they undoubtedly produced as painkillers, stimulants, and mood alterers, but they also came to require their regular use in order to maintain a sense of well-being, to "feel themselves." And, in the absence of these drugs, these dependent users suffered prolonged anxiety, restlessness, sleep disturbance, and other symptoms we now call withdrawal or the "abstinence syndrome." Sometimes called "chemical dependency," drug addiction today is defined in the standard textbooks and diagnostic manuals of both medicine and psychiatry as a *disease.*

The Disease Concept of Addiction

We now know that addictive phenomena are associated with certain drug actions within the nervous system and changes that occur in the regulation of the information that nerve signals carry—known as neurotransmission. Biologically speaking, addiction may be understood as a disorder of neurotransmission associated with the effects of such drugs (including alcohol and tobacco) on particular parts of the brain. These areas normally produce similar substances, at minute levels, that are natural versions (called ligands) of most psychoactive drugs (e.g., endorphins)—a form of the opiates. Alterations of neurotransmission involving these ligands appear to form the basis for all of the long-term and short-term effects associated with externally administered psychoactive drugs. And, in the case of addiction (according to researcher Elliot Gardner), these drugs may hijack our natural systems and begin to alter the complex and subtle processes that normally regulate neurotransmission. These changes can endure for years, and the long-lasting (chronic) nature of addiction is one of its hallmarks. This can be seen in the tenaciousness of even self-destructive drug use that the addict sincerely wishes to stop, the great difficulty many people have in stopping, and the persistence of a felt need for the drug even after periods of complete cessation—often leading to a return to drug use (relapse).

The disease model of addiction includes the development of a very specific set of problems often associated with the regular use of certain drugs; chief among them are tolerance, withdrawal, and craving.

Tolerance. With the regular use of an addictive drug, some people need more and more of the drug to produce the same effect or, conversely, get less of an effect from the same dose.

When opiates are used as painkillers for a long period, it is frequently necessary to increase the dose to produce the same analgesic effect. The regular coffee drinker may develop tolerance to caffeine and drink several cups at night without affecting his or her sleep, whereas the nontolerant coffee drinker will be up all night from a single espresso; likewise for the cigarette smoker who develops tolerance to nicotine and smokes several packs a day. With illicit drugs (whose cost is high), tolerance drives the addict to need more of the drug and to obtain more money to get enough of the drug just to feel normal (i.e., to avoid withdrawal).

Withdrawal (abstinence syndrome). This is the other face of tolerance and a clear marker of the body's memory of drug effects. In withdrawal, a regular user reacts adversely to the absence of the drug to which he or she has become tolerant. The withdrawal from most drugs has two phases: short term (acute) and long term (chronic). Withdrawal symptoms differ for the specific drug. The coffee drinker will experience headaches (which are quickly relieved by a cup or two), whereas the heroin addict, depending on the history of use, can suffer painful cramps, itching, sweating, and emotional jumpiness (once again reliably and quickly reversed by a dose of *any* opiate). But for most addictive drugs, the acute stage of withdrawal is characterized by a pervasive and highly distracting unease, often accompanied by sleep disturbance and diffuse anxiety that makes it difficult to think about much besides obtaining the drug (and instant relief). When in withdrawal, the dependent user has great difficulty in resisting the drug when it is available. The power of this need is formidable: Think about the cigarette smoker who will brave a winter storm to buy a pack in the middle of the night as an indication of the strength of what is often called "drug craving."

> *In the case of addiction . . . drugs may hijack our natural systems.*

Drug craving. If addiction can be understood as a complex set of biological cues in which the body (in essence) says, "I need this drug to feel normal," craving is the person's psychological experience and conscious awareness of that fact. It is perhaps the most important phenomenon of addiction because it motivates the addict so powerfully and for so long to use the drug in order to get relief. Although the use of a drug to feel at ease or to create a sense of well-being is not alien to most of us (think of the morning coffee or the social use of alcohol or cigarettes to relax), in the case of dependence, one does not feel normal without regular doses. And for illicit drugs, where society demands total abstinence and the drug is difficult and dangerous to obtain, this virtually dictates insufficient doses and frequent periods of prolonged craving.

Limitations of the Disease Model

But viewing addiction as a disease is a two-edged sword—useful but potentially dangerous. Its usefulness comes from the value of having a consistent physiological explanation of what are clearly powerful biological phenomena, grounded in scientific research in both pharmacology and brain functioning.

> *Where society demands total abstinence and the drug is difficult and dangerous to obtain, this virtually dictates insufficient doses and frequent periods of prolonged craving.*

However, that is not the whole story, and our biological understanding of addiction (as a disorder of neurotransmission) does not mean that the social and psychological issues in drug use and addiction are unimportant. Indeed, in an environment freighted with powerful moral and legal reactions to the use of drugs, the stigma attached to drugs may come to be a more important factor than the biology of addiction; the demonization of drugs and the criminalization of the drug user (i.e., the war on drugs) could be more damaging to the individual and society than drug use or addiction. Despite great advances in our scientific understanding of drug actions, the view of drug use and addiction as a primarily moral (and legal) problem still persists and shapes the public discourse on their meaning. These negative perceptions powerfully determine our social and political responses to addiction—usually at the expense of the biological or disease model and of the drug user. Thus, although the disease model may be in all of the medical textbooks, it is still not the basis of our overwhelmingly punitive response to the addict. Today, most addicts spend more time behind bars than in treatment for their "disease."

> *Today, most addicts spend more time behind bars than in treatment for their 'disease.'*

Another shortcoming of the disease model is that it easily overlooks the beneficial effects of many of the same drugs that it calls *pathogenic* (i.e., that are seen as the *cause* of the disease of addiction). Some form of drug use is virtually universal, and we often fail to distinguish between drug use and abuse or addiction. Although there is the potential for many drugs to produce adverse outcomes (among them addiction and toxic poisoning), these represent the minority of outcomes associated with even the use of some of the most powerful drugs, such as heroin and cocaine. And although the phenomena of addiction may be understood biologically in a disease model, this model is much less useful for understanding the full spectrum of drug use, which includes individual experimentation and recreational use, the highly structured and socialized patterns of psychoactive drug use seen in many tribal peoples, and the widespread use of alcohol in Western society. Even though alcohol use is generally accepted in our society today, we can still recognize that alcoholism is a disease and only a part (albeit an important part) of the normal pattern of use of this particular drug. At this time, we have difficulty accepting this broad range of patterns of use for the illicit drugs (like the opiates and marijuana), and we tend to forget that alcohol was prohibited in the United States from 1920 to 1934, a time when marijuana use was quite legal.

2

Addiction Is Not a Brain Disease

Jeffrey A. Schaler

Jeffrey A. Schaler is a psychologist and a teacher. He has written Addiction Is a Choice *and* Drugs: Should We Legalize, Decriminalize, or Deregulate?

The disease model of drug addiction is flawed—people choose to abuse drugs. While addiction is often considered to be a disease, it is more accurately thought of as indicative of a strong will. People willfully ignore the advice of doctors, family, and friends in their determination to use drugs or alcohol.

In its traditional definition, addiction simply means that someone likes to do something, moves toward something, or says yes to something. As [psychologists Bruce K.] Alexander and [A.R.F.] Schweighofer have pointed out, addiction can be 'positive' (good) or 'negative' (bad), drug- or non–drug related, and characterized by tolerance and withdrawal or not characterized by tolerance and withdrawal.

Tolerate refers to the fact that through continued use of a drug, or repetition of some activity, people often feel the need to 'increase the dose' to produce the kind of pleasurable experience they once had. *Withdrawal* refers to the physiological (as well as psychological) changes that occur when drug use ceases.

A positive addiction enhances the values we hold dear. Through a positive addiction we pull our life together, creating meaning and purpose. Obviously, that sense of meaning and purpose varies from person to person. A negative addiction pulls our life apart. By engaging in a negative addiction we live in conflict with ourselves, which again bears on the sense of meaning and purpose in our lives. Positive addictions may include alcohol, work, and love. Negative addictions may also include alcohol, work, and love. Addictions are as diverse as peoples' values.

The newer usage of 'addiction' to refer to drugs, loss of control, withdrawal, and tolerance, along with the theory that addiction is a disease, developed out of the moralistic rhetoric of the temperance and anti-opium movements of the nineteenth century. This restricted use of the word served several purposes, according to Alexander and Schweighofer. It was a trend of the times to medicalize social deviancy—to label those who contravened society's norms as sick and in need of treatment. Linking addiction to drugs and illness suggested it was a medical problem. This link could also be employed in an attempt to scare people away from drug use, a tactic that became increasingly important to anti-opium reformers. In its origin, the anti-opium movement was a racist anti-immigration movement, directed against West Coast Chinese, who were thought to be able to work harder because of opium and thus unfairly undercut the working conditions of Caucasian laborers.

Consider one of the most uncomfortable and difficult addictions we know of. This addiction can be either positive or negative, depending on many circumstances. It is characterized by both tolerance and withdrawal: the emotional and physical manifestations of withdrawal are frequently severe (they can be far more severe than is usually the case with heroin or cocaine). These pangs of withdrawal often lead to suicide, and withdrawal from this addiction is indeed a major cause of death among young people. The addiction is called 'love'.

On the other hand, many other people use allegedly addicting drugs (pursue romantic relationships) for long periods of time, choose to give up those drugs (love objects), and then experience virtually no symptoms of tolerance or withdrawal, let alone irresistible cravings causing them to continue to use drugs (seek out the loved one) at any expense.

The Iron Will of the Addict

The disease model credo dominates present-day drug policy. Yet some of its tenets are rejected by the great majority of addiction researchers. Taken as a package, these beliefs are somewhat contradictory: the thinking and motivation of the addict are considered to be, at the same time, both absolutely crucial and totally immaterial. Addiction is a 'disease' to be 'treated', yet 'treatment' consists of talking sessions aimed at changing the addict's beliefs and motives.

Disease-model advocates maintain that addiction cannot be controlled through an act of will: the heavy drinker or drug user has an 'impaired will'. Addiction is characterized by an inability willfully to control one's behavior, especially in relation to certain kinds of 'addictive' drugs, for example, alcohol, heroin, cocaine, or nicotine.

> *Linking addiction to drugs and illness suggested it was a medical problem.*

The opposite view is surely worth considering. Heavy drinking and drug use are characterized by strong will. The more single-mindedly self-destructive the drinker or other drug user is, the more indicative their behavior is of a strong will, even an iron will. If the term *addict* has come to imply passivity and involuntariness, a more accurate word (from the same Latin root) to describe the person who chooses a negative addiction is *dictator*. These people become dictators, of a sort, by choosing to consume alcohol and other 'addictive' drugs, possibly at the expense of family, job, and health, making themselves and other people suffer from their iron will.

Some other 'dictators' do the same with chess, bodybuilding, money-making, music, ministering to the poor, or pursuing enlightenment. We often tend to applaud those who ruthlessly subordinate their lives to an over-riding purpose we consider valuable; we often tend to boo and hiss those who ruthlessly subordinate their lives to an over-riding purpose we consider pointless, or destructive. Considered in this way, addiction becomes an ethical issue. . . .

Free-Will Model: What It Is

According to those who reject the disease model, humans are capable of deliberate action in pursuit of chosen goals. Although much human behavior is not carefully thought out, the acting person may at any moment pay more attention to such thoughtless behavior, and consciously modify it. All such voluntary human action is ultimately under conscious control, and is to be distinguished from an unconscious reflex or seizure, which is involuntary.

> **" Heavy drinking and drug use are characterized by strong will. "**

Whenever we see someone behaving in a conscious, goal-directed manner (rushing to get to the liquor store before it closes, laying in a supply of alka seltzer, and so forth) we can be sure that this behavior is not to be explained by physiology alone. Physiology alone can never determine that someone will take a drug, or how often they will take it. Part of their motivation may be to make themselves feel better, and the explanation for this may owe something to physiology. But their beliefs, values, and goals are also essential in forming their intentions.

Heavy, habitual users of drugs, including alcohol, often moderate or cease taking the drug without help from anyone else. There is no evidence that any form of 'addiction treatment' can increase the proportion of drug consumers who moderate or halt their consumption of drugs.

Individuals in the habit of taking a drug frequently or heavily may, and often do, decide to moderate or to quit. If they decide to quit, they may decide to stop suddenly or to taper off gradually. No one technique is best for everyone. Some people will be happiest reducing their intake to a modest level, others will wish to quit completely. Of the latter, some will be happiest quitting abruptly, others will prefer to gradually taper off. The notion that 'once you're an addict, you're always an addict', that an addict (or alcoholic) can never be cured but only 'in remission', is nothing but religious dogma; it does not have a shred of scientific support.

The Credo of the Free-Will Model

1. The best way to overcome addiction is to rely on your own willpower. (*You* are the 'higher power'.)
2. People can stop depending on drugs or alcohol as they develop other ways to deal with life.
3. Addiction has more to do with the environments people

live in than with the drugs they are addicted to.

4. People often outgrow drug and alcohol addiction.
5. Alcoholics and drug addicts can learn to moderate their drinking or cut down on their drug use.
6. People become addicted to alcohol and other drugs when life is going badly for them.
7. Drug addicts and alcoholics can and often do find their own ways out of their addictions, without outside help.
8. You have to rely on yourself to overcome an addiction.
9. Drug addiction is often a way of life people rely on to cope with, or avoid coping with, the world.

If you find these propositions ludicrous or outrageous, you are addicted to the disease model. I hope to persuade you to addict yourself to the truth. Switching addictions is rarely easy or painless. It takes the exercise of willpower, but you do have plenty of that.

3

The Chemical Properties of Drugs Cause Addiction

Darryl S. Inaba and William E. Cohen

Darryl S. Inaba is a professor of pharmacology at the University of California, San Francisco Medical Center. He is also chief executive officer of Haight Ashbury Free Clinics, Inc., in the San Francisco Bay Area. William E. Cohen is a communications and education consultant at the Haight Ashbury Detox Clinic.

The chemical properties of drugs interact with the body's neurotransmitters, nerve cells, and other tissues in several ways. Drug users develop tolerance of various types, including behavioral tolerance—where the brain learns to compensate for the drug's effects—and reverse tolerance—where the body loses its ability to handle drugs. The body also develops tissue dependence and the mind develops psychic dependence with prolonged drug use. Withdrawal happens when a drug user stops taking drugs after developing tolerance and tissue dependence. Because there are many different drugs—each with different chemical properties—and because each person's body reacts to drugs differently, the process of developing addiction is different for each individual.

I t is the way in which psychoactive drugs interact with neurotransmitters, nerve cells, and other tissues that helps determine how drugs affect people and why it is difficult to control their levels of use. Factors such as tolerance, tissue depen-

Darryl S. Inaba and William E. Cohen, *Uppers, Downers, All Arounders: Physical and Mental Effects of Psychoactive Drugs*. Ashland, OR: CNS Publications, 2000.

dence, psychic dependence, withdrawal, and drug metabolism can moderate or intensify these effects. . . .

Tolerance

The body regards any drug it takes as a toxin. Various organs, especially the liver and kidneys, try to eliminate the chemical before it does too much damage. But if the use continues over a long period of time, the body is forced to change and adapt to develop *tolerance* to the continued input of foreign substances. The net result is that the user has to take larger and larger amounts to achieve the same effect. In experiments with rats, one hour of access to self-administered cocaine per session did not increase intake or tolerance. However, six hours of access escalated tolerance and increased the *hedonic set point* that is defined as an individual's preferred level of pharmacological effects from a drug. For example, the body adapts to an upper, such as methamphetamine, in order to minimize the stimulant's effect on the heart and other systems, so the drug appears to weaken with each succeeding dose if it's used frequently. More has to be taken just to achieve the same effect. One amphetamine tablet on the first day of use will energize a user and trigger a euphoria that can only be matched by 20 tablets on the 100th day of use.

Some degree of tolerance develops with all psychoactive drugs. One dose of LSD on the 1st day, three on the 7th day, and nine on the 30th day might be needed to give the same psychedelic effect if the drug were taken daily. A glass of whiskey at the beginning of one's drinking career might give the same buzz as five drinks on New Year's Eve 4 years later.

The development of tolerance varies widely depending mostly on the qualities of the drug itself. But it also depends on the amount, frequency, and duration of use, the chemistry of the user, and the psychological state of mind of the user. There are several different kinds of tolerance.

Kinds of Tolerance

Dispositional Tolerance. The body speeds up the breakdown (metabolism) of the drug in order to eliminate it. This is particularly the case with barbiturates and alcohol. An example of this biological adaptation can be seen with alcohol. It increases the amount of cytocells and mitochondria in the liver that are available to neutralize the drug, therefore more has to be drunk to reach the same level of intoxication.

Pharmacodynamic Tolerance. Nerve cells become less sensitive to the effects of the drug and even produce an antidote or antagonist to the drug. With opioids, the brain will generate more opioid receptor sites and produce its own antagonist, cholecystokinin. Further, down regulation of receptor sites results in pharmacodynamic tolerance.

Behavioral Tolerance. The brain learns to compensate for the effects of the drug by using parts of the brain not affected. A drunk person can make himself appear sober when confronted by police but might be staggering again a few minutes later.

Reverse Tolerance. Initially one becomes less sensitive to the drug but as it destroys certain tissues and/or as one grows older, the trend is suddenly reversed and the user becomes less able to handle even moderate amounts. This is particularly true in alcoholics when, as the liver is destroyed, it loses the ability to metabolize the drug. An alcoholic with cirrhosis of the liver can stay drunk all day long on a pint of wine because the raw alcohol is passing through the body repeatedly, unchanged.

> *A glass of whiskey at the beginning of one's drinking career might give the same buzz as five drinks on New Year's Eve 4 years later.*

Acute Tolerance (tachyphylaxis). In these cases, the body begins to adapt almost instantly to the toxic effects of the drug. With tobacco, for example, tolerance and adaptation begin to develop with the first puff. Someone who tries suicide with barbiturates can develop an acute tolerance and survive the attempt. They could be awake and alert even with twice the lethal dose in their systems even if they've never taken barbiturates before.

Select Tolerance. If increased quantities of a drug are taken to overcome this tolerance and to achieve a certain high, it's easy to forget that tolerance to the physical side effects also continues to escalate but not at the same rate. The dose needed to achieve an emotional high comes closer and closer to the lethal physical dose of that drug.

Thus people develop different rates of tolerance to different effects of the same drug. Codeine kills pain but causes nausea on the first day it is taken. Within a week it still kills pain but no longer causes nausea.

> *"With tobacco . . . tolerance and adaptation begin to develop with the first puff."*

Inverse Tolerance (kindling). The person becomes more sensitive to the effects of the drug as the brain chemistry changes. A marijuana or cocaine user, after months of getting a minimal effect from the drug, will all of a sudden get an intense reaction. . . .

A cocaine or methamphetamine addict develops a greater risk of heart attack or stroke after prolonged use due to the toxic effects of those drugs. Thus they become more sensitive to the toxic effects after continued use.

Tissue Dependence

Tissue dependence is the biological adaptation of the body due to prolonged use of drugs. It is often quite extensive, particularly with downers. In fact with certain drugs, the body can change so much that the tissues and organs come to depend on the drug just to stay normal. If the body doesn't have the drug, its biological adaptations can cause a series of side effects. For example, the increased number of cytocells and mitochondria in the liver of an alcoholic depends on repeated use of alcohol to maintain their existence. When alcohol is discontinued, their numbers return to normal levels. Enzymatic changes in the liver of a heroin addict trigger the need for regular doses of heroin to maintain the new chemical balance. . . .

Psychic Dependence and the Reward-Reinforcing Action of Drugs

Psychic dependence and the positive reward-reinforcing action of drugs result from the direct influence of drugs on brain chemistry. Drugs cause an altered state of consciousness and distorted perceptions pleasurable to the user. These reinforce the continued use of the drug. Psychic dependence can therefore result from the continued misuse of drugs to deal with life's problems or from their continued use to compensate for inherited deficiencies in brain-reward hormones.

Drugs also have the innate ability to guide and virtually hypnotize the user into continual use (called the "positive reward-reinforcing of drugs"). In the animal experiments in which rats were trained to press a lever that would feed them heroin or other drugs intravenously, they would continue to press the lever even before physical dependence had developed, showing that a psychoactive drug, in and of itself, can reinforce the desire to use. . . .

Withdrawal

When the user stops taking a drug that has created tolerance and tissue dependence, the body is left with an altered chemistry. There might be an overabundance of enzymes, receptor sites, or neurotransmitters. Without the drug to support this altered chemistry, the body all of a sudden tries to return to normal. Withdrawal is defined as the body's attempt to rebalance itself after cessation of prolonged use of a psychoactive drug. All the things the body was kept from doing while taking the drug, it does to excess while in withdrawal. For example, consider how the desired effects of heroin are quickly replaced by unpleasant withdrawal symptoms once a long-time user stops taking the drug. . . .

There are three distinct types of withdrawal symptoms: nonpurposive, purposive, and protracted.

> *Drugs . . . have the innate ability to guide and virtually hypnotize the user into continual use.*

Nonpurposive Withdrawal. Nonpurposive withdrawal consists of objective physical signs that are directly observable upon cessation of drug use by an addict. These include seizures, sweating, goose bumps, vomiting, diarrhea, and tremors that are a direct result of the tissue dependence.

Purposive Withdrawal. Purposive withdrawal results from either addict manipulation (hence purposive or with purpose) or from a psychic conversion reaction from the expectation of the withdrawal process. Psychic conversion is an emotional expectation of physical effects that have no biological explanation. Since a common behavior of most addicts is malingering or manipulation in an effort to secure more drugs, sympathy, or money, they may claim to have withdrawal symptoms that are very diverse and difficult to verify, e.g., "My nerves are in an uproar. You've got to give me something, Doc!" Physicians and pharmacists have to be very aware of these kinds of manipulations. . . .

Within the past few decades, the portrayal of drug addiction by the media, books, movies, and television has resulted in another kind of purposive withdrawal. When they run out of drugs, younger addiction-naive drug users expect to suffer withdrawal symptoms similar to those portrayed in the media. This expectation results in a neurotic condition whereby they experience a wide range of reactions even though tissue dependence has not truly developed. Treatment personnel need to avoid overreacting to these symptoms.

> *The odor of burnt matches or burning metal . . . several months after detoxification may cause a heroin addict to suffer . . . withdrawal symptoms.*

Protracted Withdrawal (environmental triggers & cues). A major danger to maintaining recovery and preventing a drug overdose during relapse is protracted withdrawal. This is a flashback or recurrence of the addiction withdrawal symptoms and triggering of a heavy craving for the drug long after an addict has been detoxified. The cause of this reaction (similar to a posttraumatic stress phenomenon) often happens when some sensory input (odor, sight, noise) stimulates the memories experienced during drug use or withdrawal and evokes a desire for the drug by the addict. For instance, the odor of burnt matches or burning metal (smells that occur when cooking heroin) several months after detoxification may cause a heroin addict to suffer some withdrawal symptoms. Any white powder may cause craving in a cocaine addict; a blue pill may do it to a Valium® addict; and a barbecue can cause a recovering alcoholic to crave a drink.

Strangely, research with animals and interviews with addicts demonstrates that once abstinence is interrupted, both tolerance and tissue dependence develop at a much faster rate than before. . . .

Metabolism and Excretion

Metabolism is defined as the body's mechanism for processing, using, and inactivating a foreign substance, such as a drug or food in the body, while excretion is the process of eliminating those foreign substances and their metabolites from the body.

As a drug exerts its influence upon the body, it is gradually neutralized, usually by the liver. It can also be metabolized in the blood, in the lymph fluid, by brain enzymes and chemicals, or by most any body tissue that recognizes the drug as a foreign substance. Drugs can also be inactivated by diverting them to body fat or proteins that hold the substances to prevent them from acting on body organs.

The liver, in particular, has the ability to break clown or alter the chemical structure of drugs, making them less active or inert. The kidneys, on the other hand, filter the metabolites, water, and other waste from the blood and the resulting urine through the ureter, bladder, and urethra. Drugs can also be excreted out of the body by the lungs, in sweat, or in feces.

Metabolic processes generally decrease (but occasionally increase) the effects of psychoactive drugs. For instance, the liver's enzymes help convert alcohol to water, oxygen, and carbon dioxide that are then excreted from the body through the kidneys, sweat glands, and lungs. Some drugs, such as Valium®, are known as pro-drugs because they are transformed by the liver's enzymes into three or four other drugs that are more active than the original drug.

> *Some drugs . . . are transformed by the liver's enzymes into three or four other drugs that are more active than the original drug.*

If a drug is eliminated slowly, as with Valium®, it can affect the body for hours, even days. If it is eliminated quickly, as with smokable cocaine or nitrous oxide, the major actions might last just a few minutes, though other subtle side effects last for days, weeks, or even longer. Following are some other factors that affect the metabolism of drugs.

- Age: After the age of 30 and with each subsequent year, the body produces fewer and fewer liver enzymes capable of metabolizing certain drugs, thus the older the person, the greater the effect. This is especially true with drugs like alcohol and sedative-hypnotics.

- Race: Different ethnic groups have different levels of enzymes. Over 50% of Asians break down alcohol more slowly than do Caucasians. They suffer more side effects, such as redness of the face, than many other ethnic groups.

- Heredity: Individuals pass certain traits to their offspring that affect the metabolism of drugs. They can have a low level of enzymes that metabolize the drug; they can have more body fat that will store certain drugs like Valium® or marijuana; or they can have a high metabolic rate that will usually eliminate drugs more quickly from the body.

- Sex: Males and females have different body chemistry and different body water volumes. Drugs such as alcohol and barbiturates generally have greater effects in women than in men.

- Health: Certain medical conditions affect metabolism. Alcohol in a drinker with severe liver damage (hepatitis, cirrhosis) causes more problems than in a drinker with a healthy liver.

- Emotional State: The emotional state of the drug user also has a major influence on the drug's effects. LSD in people with paranoia can be very dangerous because it can further disrupt the chemical imbalance of the brain and increase their paranoia.

- Other Drugs: The presence of two or more drugs can keep the body so busy metabolizing one that metabolism of the second drug is delayed. For example, the presence of alcohol keeps the liver so busy that a Xanax® or Seconal® will remain in the body two or three times longer than normal. Other drug interactions also cause increased or decreased effects and toxicity.

- Other Factors: In addition factors such as the weight of the user, the level of tolerance, the state of mind, and even the weather can affect metabolism of a psychoactive drug.

- Exaggerated Reaction: In some cases the reaction to a drug will be out of proportion to the amount taken. Perhaps the user has an allergy to the drug in much the same way a person can go into shock from a single bee sting. For example, a person who lacks the enzyme which metabolizes cocaine can die from exposure to just a tiny amount. . . .

Side Effects

If drugs did only what people wanted them to and they weren't used to excess, they wouldn't be much of a problem. But drugs not only generate desired emotional and physical effects; they also trigger side effects that can be mild, moderate, dangerous, or sometimes fatal. This competition between the emotional/physical effects that users want and those they don't want is one of the main problems with using psychoactive drugs. For example, a psychoactive drug such as codeine (an opioid-downer) can be prescribed by a physician to relieve pain, to suppress a cough, or to treat severe diarrhea. It also acts as a sedative, gives a feeling of well-being, and induces numbness and relaxation. People who self-prescribe codeine just for the feeling of well-being or numbness will have slower reaction time and often become constipated. With moderate use they can also be subject to nausea, pinpoint pupils, dry skin, and slowed respiration. And if users keep using in order to recapture that feeling of well-being over a long period of time, they can become lethargic, lose sexual desire, and even become compulsive users of the drug. . . .

Levels of Use

It is important to judge the level at which a person uses drugs and thereby have a benchmark by which to judge whether drug use is accelerating or becoming problematic. To judge a person's level of use, it is necessary to first know the amount, frequency, and duration of psychoactive drug use. These three factors by themselves are not enough to judge the level of use. The second key factor is to know the impact the use has on an individual's life. For example, a man might drink a six-pack of lager beer (amount) twice a week (frequency) and keep it up for 12 years (duration) without developing any problems. Another man might only drink on Fridays but doesn't stop until he passes out. The second man might have more problems regarding health, the law, or money than the first man who drinks every evening but functions well on the job and works at his relationships. . . .

Unfortunately with most psychoactive drugs, a point is

passed where it becomes harder and harder for the person to choose the level at which they want to continue to use. That point can vary radically from person to person. . . .

Recent archival research by the Office of National Drug Control Policy has shown that those who experiment with alcohol, nicotine, and marijuana between the ages of 10–12 are tremendously more likely to become a heroin or cocaine addict than those who don't. Further, their research demonstrates that those individuals who never try nicotine before the age of 21 have almost zero addiction to tobacco later in life.

4

Psychological Factors, Not the Chemical Properties of Drugs, Cause Addiction

Lance M. Dodes

Lance M. Dodes is an assistant clinical professor of psychiatry at Harvard Medical School. He is a psychiatrist and psychoanalyst and is the director of the Boston Center for Problem Gambling.

Not everyone who uses drugs is predisposed to true addiction. While a drug may cause physical addiction, if the right psychological factors are not there, the drug user will not become truly addicted. If the addiction is only physical, then quitting is much easier. It is the psychological factors—such as an inability to function well in difficult situations—not the physical ones that make quitting drugs so hard and relapse so frequent. Once people become aware of the psychological reasons for their addictions, quitting becomes easier.

W hen American soldiers were in Vietnam, many of them used heroin or other narcotics both because they were readily available and because they were in an extraordinarily stressful setting. Heroin and similar narcotics, of course, are famous for being physically addictive, producing tolerance, physical withdrawal symptoms, and cravings for the drug, which are part of the withdrawal process. Of the soldiers who used these drugs, many took enough to produce physical addiction. The interesting thing is what happened to these men when they returned to the United States. When they were studied [according to L. Robins, J. Helzer, and D. Davis] "usage and addiction essentially decreased to pre-Vietnam levels." Indeed, even among men who continued to use some narcotics, "the susceptibility to addiction declined dramatically. About one half of all narcotics users in Vietnam had become addicted, whereas only 7% of users after return became addicted at any time during the post-Vietnam period. This . . . produced addiction remission rates of 95% for those who had been addicted in Vietnam, rates of remission unheard of among narcotics addicts treated in the United States [according to the same study]." How did these soldiers escape being "hooked"? The narcotics were certainly strong enough.

> *Practically none of the patients in these programs stayed clean from drugs after detoxification.*

At the time these results were published, they were astounding to many people who had worked in heroin detoxification centers. Nobody had predicted this result, because detoxifying people from narcotics in the United States had been so ineffective. Practically none of the patients in these programs stayed clean from drugs after detoxification.

In comparing the results of the veterans study with the results from heroin detoxification centers in the United States, one conclusion seems evident. Since both groups used the same substances, the difference in results must have been because the people were different. What this means is that nearly all of the returning men who had used narcotics did not continue to be addicted because, while they had used large amounts of physically addictive drugs, *they* were not predisposed to addiction.

Addiction Is a Human Problem

The results of this study of Vietnam veterans underscores a basic point. *Addiction is a human problem that resides in people, not*

nowhere near being the central one.

Nor does physical addiction play a significant role in *relapse* to addiction after a period of abstinence, as with the large number of people who return to an addiction even years after being physically withdrawn from a drug. Yet, it is relapse that is the real practical problem with addiction. The old joke, "It's easy to quit, I've done it a hundred times," reflects the fact that nearly everyone who suffers with an addiction does stop at one time or another. But unless the emotional factors that originally led to the addiction are addressed, relapse is the rule. Indeed, the original causes of an addiction and the causes for relapse are fundamentally the same psychological factors—which is why exploring the reappearance of urges to perform an addictive act can be so helpful to understanding the roots of an addiction. And after the relatively short period of physical withdrawal, physical addiction has little to do with this.

> *Many were physically addicted to cigarettes, yet . . . they were able to quit.*

If you have an addiction to a drug, it may have seemed to you that physical factors are more important than this because you have come to worry about whether you can get along without the physical effect of a drug. In other words, you may feel that you have been self-prescribing for practical reasons to function better—as in using alcohol to remove social inhibitions. In fact, people often take drugs for just this kind of reason, but this is quite different from an addiction. Self-prescription is not driven by the same intense qualities that are present in addiction and consequently is much easier to manage. . . .

Why Physical Factors Are Overemphasized

Given all the circumstances in which physical addiction is present without psychological addiction, and vice versa, why have they been so blurred together?

The most obvious reason, of course, is that the term "addiction" has been used to describe both, without any sense of the distinction between them. It would be good if these often mutually exclusive conditions were described by different words. A helpful convention would be to use the word "addiction" to mean only true or psychological addiction, and to specify "physical addiction" when speaking of that very specific phenomenon. This is the convention that I use . . .

Another root for the misplaced emphasis on physical factors in addiction has been popular reports about changes in neurotransmitter levels associated with certain commonly abused drugs. For instance, cocaine produces increased brain levels of the neurotransmitter dopamine, which leads in turn to a feeling of euphoria. After sufficient cocaine use, dopamine levels become depleted, leading to a depressed mood and cravings for more cocaine. This is the kind of thing that is often erroneously reported in the media as important in understanding the nature of addiction. However, it is simply a description of the physical addiction aspect of cocaine use; it is the old confusion of physical addiction with addiction, again.

Another basis for physical factors having been so overstated is the frequent reporting about localization of the effects of drugs in certain areas of the brain. With modern visualization techniques, it is possible to show exactly what parts of the brain are affected by the presence of a particular drug. One area that has attracted a great deal of attention, for instance, is a region of the brain called the nucleus accumbens. Popular articles that describe these localization studies often relate how a drug may affect biological activity in the particular area of the brain known to be affected—again, via altering levels of neurotransmitters that are active in that region. The new information arising from these studies, however, only describes where in the brain drugs work. It does not say anything about why people are compelled to take them, or why some people—whose brains are affected in the same areas by the drugs—do not use them addictively. Hence, while we are learning more all the time about the way drugs affect the brain, this does not provide any evidence for a physical, biochemical cause of addiction. Indeed, there is simply no evidence of any neurochemical or neuroanatomical deficit in people that accounts for their having or developing an addiction.

Historical Reasons

There is also a historical reason why physical and true addiction have been so blurred: the most commonly thought of addictions have always been drug addictions, especially alcoholism, and frequently the people suffering with these drug addictions *also* have had a physical addiction. Perhaps if, centuries ago, the first conditions recognized as addictions had been nondrug behaviors, if people had first applied the word "addiction" to behaviors such as compulsive gambling, then physical dependence wouldn't have seemed so central to the problem of addiction.

> *It is relapse that is the real practical problem with addiction.*

But to see the link between drug and nondrug addictions, or to see the psychological basis for drug addictions, would have required a psychological perspective, a level of psychological sophistication about human behavior, that has not been available throughout most of history. Aside from the works of great writers, like Shakespeare, who have shown the depth of psychological conflict that can lie behind actions, viewing behavior in psychological terms at all is a very new development in the story of mankind. The serious study of human psychology is, after all, only about a hundred years old. Those who came before that development can hardly be blamed for believing that the physical effects that they could easily see were the basis for addiction.

Today, however, watching those movies in which people are craving alcohol or heroin and are obtaining immediate relief from their withdrawal symptoms when they get their drug "fix," we can understand that what is being shown is not the *cause* of the addiction. What is being shown is a *result*, an end product of the addiction that began with a need to perform an addictive behavior—in this case, using a drug.

There are other reasons for the survival of the notion that addiction is a physical problem. Indeed, if you suffer with an addiction yourself, you are very aware of what I am about to say. All too often people suffering with addictions feel that they are bad or weak because of their addiction. Moreover, we live in a culture that frequently treats people with addictions as if their problem were caused by a moral deficiency. The idea that addiction is a physical problem may, then, provide some relief from guilt and shame. Understandably, this serves as a powerful reason to hold on to this idea, even though, like the idea that addiction is a moral deficiency, it is not true.

Finally, another reason that some people reject a psychological explanation of addiction is because they think that to say something is caused by psychological factors means it is a question of willpower—and that they are being told they are lacking in willpower. The opposite, of course, is the case. The essence of human psychology lies in not simply what is in awareness, but also the unconscious thoughts, conflicts, and feelings that drive much of our behavior, *especially* actions that are problematic and irrational. Ironically, and sadly, when people reject a psychological explanation because they confuse this with a challenge to their willpower, they do not permit themselves the relief from unrealistic self-blame that would come with truly understanding what drives their addictive behaviors.

5

Genetics Play a Key Role in Addiction

Terry Burnham and Jay Phelan

Terry Burnham is a visiting scholar at Harvard Business School. Jay Phelan is a biology professor at the University of California at Los Angeles.

Drugs work on the body's evolutionary reward system, which encourages people to use drugs repeatedly. The human body is genetically programmed to pass along its genes to the next generation. For this reason, sex is pleasurable. Unfortunately, the reward centers that make people enjoy sex can be hijacked by drugs. Drugs also make people feel good, and such pleasure encourages further drug use, sometimes even addiction. Studies have found that many people are genetically predisposed to enjoy drug use more than others, and are therefore more prone to addiction.

Can the actions of a few brain cells really influence our mood or behavior? In the 1950s, a psychologist surgically implanted electrodes in rats' brains and stimulated them. Usually, sending a tiny current of electricity elicited little response. Positioning the buzzing electrodes near a part of the brain called the hypothalamus, however, seemed to make the rats happy. Actually that's the understatement of the year. Stimulating the hypothalamus made them ecstatic.

Subsequent experiments have shown that if the electric reward is doled out only when the rat accomplishes something—learns to navigate part of a maze, for example—the rat works at the task eagerly until it is mastered, craving the reward. As long as the rewards keep coming, the little rodents keep working, even to the point of mastering complex mazes that humans would find nearly impossible.

It's not the learning that they love. When the same rats are allowed to self-administer this brain stimulation they forget about the mazes, forget about their friends, and forget about pretty much everything else. They sit, pressing the lever a hundred times a minute for hours on end. They won't even take meal breaks, choosing to press the lever when they are famished and continuing until they die of starvation.

Genes and the Reward System

What would we do if we could stimulate a similarly intense pleasure center in our own brains? This question isn't hypothetical, of course, because we can. Consider the mother of all pleasure pathways: the orgasm. The positive sensation we feel is the release of chemicals that stimulate the same part of the brain that makes rats so happy. These "do-it-again" centers, when activated, associate pleasure with whatever behavior caused the brain stimulation.

Think of a do-it-again center as a square slot in your brain. Having sex is like discovering the proper square peg to fit the slot. It makes us happy. The reward is an orgasm and this creates the desire to repeat the behavior, sex in this case. Having discovered the square peg to the magic kingdom, we want to do it again. (And again. And again.)

> *Our genes want us to perform a variety of behaviors and accordingly have built many do-it-again centers.*

While we are busy enjoying our orgasms, our genes are laughing all the way to the Darwinian bank. From their perspective, the result is (or was for our ancestors before birth control) having babies, which means the genes have successfully made it into the next generation.

In their quest for immortality, our genes want us to perform a variety of behaviors and accordingly have built many do-it-again centers: imagine round and oval and star-shaped slots permeating your brain. Genetically favorable behaviors have been linked to these slots.

> **❝** *Our brain's signaling system can be . . . tricked—with disastrous consequences.* **❞**

Eating a bit of strawberry shortcake, we are rewarded with happiness as a round peg fills the round, calorie-seeking slot. Achieving victory over a rival, we feel the euphoria that reliably accompanies a star-shaped peg filling the star-shaped status slot. In actuality, the variously shaped pegs are brain chemicals that stimulate the do-it-again centers.

In creating such a pleasure system, our genes have built a reward system in which our pursuit of happiness accomplishes their goals. No one has a baby because they want to replicate genes, but by merely seeking pleasure and avoiding pain we unconsciously further our genes' goals. We needn't be aware of genes at all; merely engaging in certain behaviors makes us feel good and want to do them again.

Drugs and the Reward System

Drugs hijack and short-circuit this evolutionary reward system. Our ancestors got their chemical kicks the old-fashioned way: they earned them through good behavior. With drugs, our pleasure centers can be stirred without the essential behaviors at all. How do drugs hijack the pain and pleasure mutes in our brains?

We need to recognize that our only true erogenous zones are in our brains. In some completely paralyzed men, for instance, it is possible to stimulate the genitals to produce erections and even ejaculations. These patients, however, find no satisfaction because their brains never get the message. The same patients can, however, experience sensations like orgasms if the pleasure centers of their brains are stimulated. The trouble is, the brain has to be signaled about our behavior through the nervous system, and any signaling system can be manipulated.

Consider, for example, how predators lethally exploit the signaling system of the firefly. If you sit in a field on a summer night, you may be treated to a whirl of fireflies flashing in the dark. This dance is not for our pleasure; they are performing a mating ritual. It's pitch black in the field, and many different species are flying around. The flies need to find members of their own species in order to mate successfully, so they use a special Morse code signaling system that says, "Hey, I'm your type and I'm ready for action."

The fireflies don't actually see their potential lovers but instead communicate with belly lights. One species may beckon with two long flashes and a short while another may use four shorts followed by a long. When a sexually charged fly detects the right series of flashes, he or she swoops in, ready to begin a family.

Some of these flying Romeos and Juliets receive a rude shock. Arriving at the signaler, tiny loins aflame, they find jaws of death, not arms of love. Devious predators take advantage of the signaling system by producing the exact sequence of flashes sent by a willing mate. When a fly comes a-courtin' at the wrong home, it's dinnertime for the talented predator.

Our brain's signaling system can be similarly tricked—with disastrous consequences. When we do something good, our pleasure is caused by chemicals called neurotransmitters that stimulate our brains' do-it-again centers. Drugs—whether recreational or therapeutic, whether found in nature or made in the laboratory—mimic neurotransmitters. Just as firefly predators duplicate the flashes of a real mate, drugs "look" just like our natural chemical signals. Remember, caffeine works because it is so similar to adenosine.

When we take a pleasure-causing drug, our brain acts as if appropriately released neurotransmitters were flooding the system. The brain thinks we have done something great, such as finding food or warmth, when in fact we may be crouched over a filthy toilet with a hypodermic of heroin in our arm. Our pleasure centers know only that they are bathed in a precise set of chemical signals that induce bliss. . . .

The Fast-Flush Response

Isabella joins her friends in sipping wine during a dinner party. As the meal progresses, her companions become tipsy. Their conversations turn racy, their moods relaxed. They refill their glasses, reveling in a little buzz. Not so for Isabella. Before her first glass is empty, she experiences a "fast-flush" response: her face turns crimson, her heart begins to race, and her head starts to pound. Worse still, she soon feels the need to vomit.

How can people respond so differently to booze? Fast-flushers like Isabella have a genetic difference that causes the buildup of a poisonous chemical called acetaldehyde. When we splash a bit of alcohol down the hatch, our bodies do a little two-step dance in which they manhandle the alcohol molecules, converting them from their intoxicating form into innocuous atoms.

> *A third of the people who smoked had an unusual copy of an important gene.*

Isabella's body adeptly starts the normal breakdown of alcohol, but she was born with defective genetic instructions for making an enzyme that disposes of the poisonous compound. One by one, the alcohol molecules are processed, but without the correct machinery, poisonous acetaldehyde accumulates. Hence the "fast-flush" reaction.

Isabella's messed-up enzyme is called aldehyde dehydrogenase, and fully half of Asian people have the same genetic mistake. But hold on. Perhaps we ought to call this mistake a molecular godsend. In a study of thirteen hundred alcoholics in Japan, guess how many were fast-flushers? *Not one.* Although half the Japanese are fast-flushers, there was not a single one among these alcoholics. A minor change in their genetic code helps them resist the lure of alcohol.

Genes and Alcoholism

So certain inborn genetic differences result in a decreased desire for drink. Is the opposite true as well? Do some individuals have genetic endowments that give them an unhealthy passion for the stuff? Animal studies suggest that this may be true.

Generally, mammals—from wild primates to household pets—avoid alcohol; given a choice, they choose water. Some scientists set out to breed rats with a taste for liquor. Each generation, only those animals with the least aversion for alcohol were selected as breeders. The rest, allowed no babies, remained heirless. The scientists soon had a rat population that loved to drink.

Interestingly, these alcohol-loving rats produced abnormally small amounts of the happy neurotransmitter serotonin in their brain. Their preference for alcohol may be an attempt to bump their serotonin levels back up to those maintained by normal rats. This finding opens a messy can of worms.

Do human drug addictions and dependencies reflect differences in our genes? Recent data suggest that they might. One group of scientists examining brains during autopsies found that the alcoholics had fewer dopamine receptors than the non-alcoholics.

Genes and Other Addictions

Genes are implicated in other addictions, too. In one study of 283 individuals, a third of the people who smoked had an unusual copy of an important gene whereas almost none of the non-smokers carried it. This gene, labeled D2, enables the pleasure centers of our brains to light up when tickled by dopamine. Smokers with the unusual form of the D2 gene produce a third fewer dopamine receptors than normal.

Given dopamine's central role in orchestrating the pleasure centers of the brain, any alteration in this system wreaks havoc on the body's natural ability to regulate and achieve happiness. Many smokers can be viewed as medicating themselves in an attempt to stimulate their dopamine systems more aggressively. By smoking they can light up their pleasure centers to the level naturally enjoyed by the non-smokers. . . .

Other drugs, too—notably cocaine—prime the body's dopamine system. The same renegade D2 gene that predisposes people to smoking is also linked with other drug addictions and even to overeating.

> *Identical twins show similar—but not identical—propensities for drug use.*

In 1997 a man in North Carolina, Thomas Richard Jones, was tried for causing the death of two women in a car accident while he was under the influence of alcohol, painkillers, and antidepressants. Noting a long history of addiction, Jones's defense attorney pleaded that "the devil lurking in this alcohol and in these pills would not turn loose of him." One of the devil's aliases may be dopamine.

This is the danger in having a brain that uses chemical signals like dopamine and serotonin to regulate pleasure and happiness. Genetic glitches in the production of these chemicals may sentence some people to lives spent in search of a chemical high.

> *Every person has strong, instinctual cravings for destructive substances.*

While genes have thus been shown to play a role in smoking, drinking, and the use of other drugs, we have clear evidence that genetic factors are not the whole story. Identical twins show similar—but not identical—propensities for drug use. If a person has a problem with alcohol, an identical twin is 25%–40% more likely than a fraternal twin to exhibit the same behavior. If genes were the whole story, identical twins would have identical behaviors.

These are the early days of understanding our brain's signaling systems. A complete understanding of addiction must incorporate both genes and the large set of non-genetic forces pushing people into or away from drug use.

Genes and Quitting Drugs

"Just say no" to drugs is the simplest way to kick a habit. Unfortunately, this obvious and low-cost approach is also the route most likely to fail. For example, in any given year only one person quits smoking for every twenty who attempt to just say no. Raw willpower seems like a great solution right up until weakness strikes and we light up a cigarette or mix a margarita.

Alcoholics Anonymous and similar programs can be viewed as super-duper, augmented willpower. They provide members with a complex support system, but at their core, success relies on individual restraint. Even twelve-step willpower doesn't work very well. Critics say just 5% of AA members stay sober for a year. Supporters of AA dispute the 95% failure rate, but whatever the exact figures, willpower provides no magic solution.

Our willpower failures are demoralizing. Surely, we feel, if we get tougher, we can stay clean. Furthermore, we are often surrounded by people who do not understand addiction. Fourteen percent of Americans will, at some point, have a serious problem with alcohol. As stunning as this number is, it also means that 86% of Americans will never have such a dependency. This disapproving majority appears to say that clean living requires just a New Year's resolution and a bit of moral courage.

The inability to control drug passions lies not in personality defects, but in the strength of our urges. For some the desire is overwhelming. The golfer John Daly was willing to pay three million dollars for a drink. Thomas Covington, a crack addict who was arrested thirty-one times, said he used drugs in spite of imprisonment and fines because "once that compulsion is there, it doesn't matter what the penalty or the threat is."

Far from being an act of pure volition, addiction has powerful evolutionary and biological roots. Subtle differences in our brain wiring make us more or less susceptible to chemical manipulation. Although our weaknesses vary and most of us are spared the extremes of John Daly and Thomas Covington, every person has strong, instinctual cravings for destructive substances.

Because drugs hijack our genetic pleasure pathways, the substance abuse battle we fight is with ourselves. When our neurons experience the euphoria of a dopamine bath following the inhalation of a dopamine reuptake inhibitor like cocaine, our brain is in heaven. Never mind that we know we shouldn't be doing drugs or that part of us doesn't want to do drugs. It's like rewarding a puppy with petting and a big bone each time she urinates on the couch. Do you think she's going to learn to pee outdoors?

Quitting drugs can be similarly challenging. Like instructing ourselves to stop wanting food or love, our brains just can't take such a command seriously—to stop the behavior that generates our brain's highest reward. So we can't possibly be surprised that willpower alone is rarely sufficient; we shouldn't just try to "handle" an addiction that is taking over our lives.

For those who have never tried drugs, abstinence may indeed be the best strategy. This is particularly true for people who have a family history of addiction. It's easier never to start than to quit. But for those who are addicted, "just say no" just won't cut it. Fortunately for them, science is looking for ways to help.

6

Addiction Is Learned

David P. Friedman and Sue Rusche

David P. Friedman is director of the Center for the Integration of Substance Abuse Research at Wake Forest University School of Medicine in Winston-Salem, North Carolina. Sue Rusche is executive director of National Families in Action (NFIA), which she cofounded in 1977. NFIA helps families prevent drug abuse.

Addiction develops through learning processes. When a person takes a drug after a stressful day, for example, and instantly feels better, that individual learns that the drug gets rid of bad feelings. This learning process encourages the person to use drugs whenever he or she feels bad, thus fueling addiction.

Much of what happens along the road from drug experimentation to drug addiction is learning, and with each stage of the addictive process a great deal of learning takes place. To understand what this means, let's look at how we learn and at how the knowledge that we acquire shapes our behavior.

Nearly every form of human behavior involves some kind of learning. Learning is the way we gather knowledge about our world. Once we have stored that knowledge, it is *memory.* Specific brain processes carried out in identifiable brain circuits allow us to take in information from our environment, store that information in memory, and retrieve it when we need it. What we learn from our environment plays a crucial role in how we behave. . . .

Learning occurs in two fundamental forms: conscious and unconscious. With *conscious learning,* which psychologists also call *explicit learning*, we use our senses to find out what is in the world and where and when events have occurred. We take in information about what we see, hear, smell, taste, and touch, and our brain stores that information in its short-term, or *working*, memory. Our brain's working memory allows us to retain information long enough to perceive it, use it, perhaps mull it over a bit, and then either store or discard it. . . .

If you use a computer, you've probably written a short note or memo, e-mailed or printed it, and then closed the document without saving it. You kept the information on the screen (and in the computer's "short-term," or buffer memory) long enough to use (send or print) it. Then, when the information was no longer useful, you discarded it, much like your short-term memory does. On the other hand, after you've entered an important document on the screen, you save it to the hard drive so you can retrieve it later. Just as your computer transfers your document from its buffer memory to its hard drive, your brain can transfer important information from your short-term memory to your long-term memory.

> *We store memories because they are accompanied by a strong emotion.*

Our *long-term memory* is like information stored on a hard drive. We can recall at will information that we use frequently, like people's names, or information that we have not used for a long time, like our street address from childhood. We use some things frequently, like the names of our children, and we have therefore learned them well. Studying to pass a test is the process of using some information just frequently enough to store it. Other times, we store memories because they are accompanied by a strong emotion. For example, almost everyone who is old enough remembers where he or she was when the *Challenger* exploded and when President Kennedy and Martin Luther King were killed.

In addition, we remember important personal events that aroused particularly strong emotions and were especially meaningful to us, though perhaps not to most other people— our wedding, the birth of a child, the death of a family member, and similar milestones. . . .

[The] powerful memory of early drug experiences is one of the things that drives users to keep taking drugs. They keep trying to duplicate the memory of those first few highs.

Short-Term Versus Long-Term Memory

There are crucial differences between short-term memory and long-term memory with respect to the brain. With *short-term memory*, information coming in from the outside world circulates along a complex brain pathway, which begins at the sensory cortex and passes through the hippocampus. The hippocampus sends the information on to the prefrontal cortex. Neuroscientists believe that rather than stopping in the cortex, incoming information flows continuously along this circuit until it is discarded.

With *long-term memory*, instead of briefly circulating the information, the brain fixes the information in the cerebral cortex. It now appears that long-term memories are laid down in the same parts of the cortex where they are first perceived. Thus, the memory of the sight of an apple would be stored in the visual cortex, but the memory of its taste would be stored in the part of the cortex where we process information from our taste buds. Understanding how the brain stores memories is one of the great quests of neuroscience. There is now considerable agreement about where in the brain this takes place (at least for vision), but precisely how the process works is still mostly a mystery.

> *[The] powerful memory of early drug experiences is one of the things that drives users to keep taking drugs.*

Most neuroscientists believe that the neurons in the long-term memory circuit probably undergo some form of structural change almost certainly at their synapses. Under the proper circumstances, neurons may generate new dendrites, axon terminals, receptors, and other components of the synapse to strengthen their connections to one another and thus increase the effectiveness of synaptic transmission. The best bet right now is that increased effectiveness of synaptic transmission underlies long-term memory.

Disruption or Destruction of Memory

It is important to understand where the brain stores memories for a number of reasons having to do with drug use. Marijuana disrupts the hippocampus and therefore disrupts short-term memory. The disruption appears to end as the drug is eliminated from the blood, but while the person is intoxicated, and probably for a few hours thereafter, the drug impairs short-term memory. If information fails to remain in short-term memory, the brain cannot reliably transfer it to long-term memory. . . .

Severe alcoholism, in which the drinker consumes large amounts of alcohol for many years, can produce a brain disorder called *Wernicke-Korsakoff's syndrome.* This disease damages some of the brain circuitry needed to create new memories and so disrupts the process that puts new information into long-term memory. This impairment is not limited to periods of intoxication. In extreme cases, people with this disorder can never learn anything new again.

Patients with Wernicke-Korsakoff's syndrome have been studied for many years. One such patient, a man in his 50s, had been addicted to alcohol all of his adult life. You could engage him in a fairly long conversation, and, after being introduced, he would repeatedly refer to you by name. He could also recall all sorts of memories from childhood and early adulthood, but nothing from the later part of his adult life after alcohol had destroyed his ability to store new information. If you were to leave the room during a conversation with him and then return a few minutes later, this patient would stare blankly at you and ask, "Who are you?" Because he no longer had the ability to store new memories, he could not remember ever seeing you. He could keep information in *working memory* while he was using it, but things just disappeared from his awareness forever not long after they were out of sight or out of the present.

Learning Can Help or Hurt

Basically, structural changes in the synapse that enable people to learn and retain what they've learned can be good or bad. People who proceed down a fairly normal path of development throughout childhood and adolescence can learn many behaviors that help them get the things that they want—a good job, meaningful relationships, and the ability to enjoy and appreciate the subtle pleasures of life. They can live out their lives in positive ways and even help better their world. But people also have the capacity to learn *maladaptive behaviors*. These behaviors are as difficult to unlearn as the adaptive behaviors would be, but the need to unlearn them is one reason addiction is such a difficult disorder to treat.

Implicit Learning and Memory

Drug users learn lots of maladaptive behaviors. They acquire some of them through the kind of learning we have just described, that is, through conscious, explicit learning. But they also acquire them through a second kind of learning, *unconscious* or *implicit learning*. Implicit learning shapes our behavior, in some ways much more profoundly than conscious learning, but we are not aware that we are learning while the process is taking place. One kind of implicit learning teaches us how to do things (as opposed to what they are or when they happened). Other kinds of learning teach us to associate a stimulus either with another stimulus or with a behavior. These kinds of learning take place through repetition. Although they take practice, that's all they take. . . .

Operant Conditioning

Operant conditioning teaches us to link a stimulus and a behavior. Although we are not aware that we are learning this relationship, we learn it all the same. Operant conditioning's teaching method is reward, and its best teaching tool is good feelings. It reinforces what we do by making us feel pleasure. For example:
- We do something (behavior).
- It makes us feel good (reward).
- We do it again (repeat behavior).

The reward reinforced the behavior. The more the behavior is reinforced, the more likely we are to repeat it. Thus, we gradually learn to repeat behaviors that make us feel good.

Positive and Negative Reinforcement

Natural reinforcers, like food and sex, are *primary reinforcers*. They directly produce positive reinforcement, with no learning or intervening steps required. Drugs do this as well. *Secondary reinforcers* produce reward, but not as directly. Their value as a reinforcer has to be learned. Money is a secondary reinforcer. Valueless by itself, you can't eat or inject it, money has immense power to motivate people. For some, being thin is a secondary reinforcer; for others, it is having a muscular body. These secondary reinforcing properties can also support drug use. For example, smoking cigarettes helps keep people thin. If they give up smoking, they will gain weight, an undesirable outcome. Men especially, but women too, abuse anabolic steroids because the bulked-up muscular look these drugs help to produce is a secondary reinforcer. It may be that people abuse hallucinogens because of their secondary reinforcing properties. These drugs relieve boredom and enhance emotionality. These effects are not primary reinforcers, but desirable for some people nonetheless.

> *Marijuana disrupts the hippocampus and therefore disrupts short-term memory.*

The reward produced by primary reinforcers is called *positive reinforcement* because it produces feelings of pleasure. Operant conditioning can also take place if bad feelings like anxiety, stress, or pain are removed. When this happens, the reward is called *negative reinforcement.*
• We feel bad.
• We do something (behavior).
• It alleviates the bad feelings (negative reinforcement).
• The next time we feel bad, we do it again.
Negative reinforcement increases the likelihood that the behavior that relieved the bad feelings will be repeated. The learning process is the same whether the reward is positive reinforcement or negative reinforcement. Positive and negative reinforcement are two sides of the same operant conditioning coin.

We can see how positive and negative reinforcement works when we think about very young children. When a child gets tired or frustrated, he often starts to cry (behavior). His mother or father picks him up and comforts him, relieving his distress and making him feel better (reinforcement). The next time the child feels distress, he cries again (repeats the behavior). He's learning a relationship between crying and getting attention, and the relief he gets when mom or dad pick him up is the tool teaching him this lesson.

Similar lesson plans teach babies how to get fed when they

are hungry, and, when they get much older, teach them to have sex in order to perpetuate the species. Think about the first time you kissed someone and felt the stirring of sexual desire.

- You kissed someone (behavior).
- It made you feel wonderful (reward).
- You kissed again (repeat the behavior).

As you explored the additional steps that ultimately lead to having sex, the good feelings they produced led you to repeat these newfound behaviors as often as possible. You do something. It makes you feel good. You do it again.

Where Operant Conditioning Occurs: The Brain Reward System

Through operant conditioning, our brain teaches us to do things that help us get food to eat, liquids to drink, sex to create the next generation, and all the other things we must do to ensure our own survival and that of our species. Operant conditioning is so important that it is linked to a special neural circuit within the brain's limbic system. When we do something to activate this circuit, it teaches us to repeat that behavior by releasing a cascade of neurotransmitters that suffuse us with feelings of pleasure. Because it does this, many people call it the *pleasure circuit*. Scientists call it the *reward circuit*, or *reward system*. Anything that turns this system on reinforces the very behavior that turned it on in the first place. We learn to do things that turn on our brain reward system.

> *Operant conditioning teaches us to link a stimulus and a behavior.*

Although the kind of learning that operant conditioning teaches us takes place all the time, we are almost always unaware of it. But we can see how it works in the laboratory when we teach a rat to press a bar to obtain food. Bar pressing is not something rats living in the wild typically do. But once a rat accidentally presses the bar in a training situation and obtains a food reward, its interest in the bar increases. The rat is not quite aware of what it did, but it understands that being near the bar produced food. Simply by spending more time near the bar, it is more likely to press it again. A few accidental presses that produce food reinforce the rat's interest in the bar again, until it learns that pressing the bar is the behavior that produces a food pellet. Then, a hungry rat will spend lots of time working on that bar.

The same is true for people. We often use the technique of operant conditioning to get people to do what we want them to do. If they do something for us, we give them a reward. It may be as simple as a "thank you" or as powerful as money. We teach children to behave well by giving them praise and sometimes special treats when they exhibit good behavior. . . .

Drugs Teach People to Take More Drugs

The absolute stunning thing about drugs of abuse is this: they turn on the reward system directly. No trial-and-error effort is required. Unlike all the natural rewards, such as food and sex, which activate this system subtly, slowly, and indirectly by first activating other brain structures, drugs activate the reward system directly. Positive reinforcement can be rapid and powerful: if natural reinforcers turn on a light, drugs set off fireworks. Drugs have the power to do this because they mimic or alter the actions of the brain's neurotransmitters in our reward system. And, instead of turning the reward system on subtly like a natural reinforcer would, drugs flood in and do it with a jolt. The direct effect of the drug on this system causes reward. Thus, through operant conditioning, *drugs reinforce drug-taking.* Nothing else has to happen. By activating this neural circuit, instead of teaching people to pursue survival, drugs threaten their survival *by teaching them to take more drugs.* . . .

Classical Conditioning

Another form of implicit learning, *classical conditioning*, builds on the foundation of operant conditioning. Classical conditioning teaches drug users to associate ordinary things and events with drug use. Over time, these ordinary things can provoke craving, intensifying the motivation to take more drugs. . . .

Cues

Classical conditioning teaches drug users to associate ordinary things such as talking on the telephone with the act of drug-taking. For example, when Sybil first started smoking, she often lit up a cigarette while talking on the phone. Gradually, Sybil unconsciously learned to associate talking on the phone with smoking a cigarette. After a while, the association became so strong that every time she answered or made a phone call, Sybil wanted a cigarette. For Sybil, a phone call became a stimulus, more commonly called a *cue* or *trigger*, which actually provoked craving for nicotine. Without ever realizing what had happened, she satisfied that craving by lighting up. Drug users develop dozens of cues that work to motivate them to keep taking drugs. Many cocaine users roll up a $10, $20, or $100 bill and snort the drug into their nostrils through this expensive tube. They learn to associate a neutral piece of paper—a $10 bill—with the act of snorting cocaine and the feelings the drug evokes. After a while, the sight of a rolled-up bill becomes a cue that provokes a craving for cocaine in these drug users. In fact, because drug addicts constantly need money to buy the drugs to which they are addicted, the sight of any money can provoke craving. . . .

> **"** *Instead of turning the reward system on subtly like a natural reinforcer would, drugs flood in and do it with a jolt.* **"**

Thus, through classical conditioning, drug users unconsciously learn to associate drug-taking with many ordinary, everyday things. Classical conditioning does not cause addiction. It is a form of learning that occurs while people are on the road to addiction. The triggers in developing addicts are not particularly strong, and they use drugs whether or not their secret triggers are activated. As time goes on, triggers add power to the urge to use drugs, but while drug use continues, the more powerful forces of reward and withdrawal control the addict's behavior. . . .

Addiction: The Sum of Many Kinds of Learning

We now know that repeated drug use changes the brain. Addictive drugs that people use exert their effects through their direct actions on axon terminals, receptors, and other parts of the synapse. And learning reinforces these changes and even gives them their meaning (implications for behavior). This learning uses the same neural circuits and processes as the learning we acquire under normal circumstances. Like any lesson well learned, it remains long after the teacher has left the classroom and the student has graduated.

> **"** *Because drug addicts constantly need money to buy the drugs to which they are addicted, the sight of any money can provoke craving.* **"**

Addicts, who have advanced degrees in drug use, have retained explicitly learned memories of powerful early drug experiences. They have learned about the rewarding effects of drugs. By repeatedly practicing this lesson, they have powerfully reinforced it. Moreover, addicts have acquired an impressive repertoire of unconscious, classically conditioned responses that will make them crave drugs when exposed to certain environmental stimuli—stimuli that have no special meaning for nonaddicts. In effect, the learning processes that we must undertake to survive have been commissioned to help addicts learn behaviors to get drugs into the body on a regular basis, no matter what obstacles might be in the way. These behaviors are maladaptive for anyone who wants to live a normal life.

The learning of maladaptive behaviors is another key aspect of addiction. It is a difficult task to learn to be a functional adult with flexible responses to complex and painful personal and social situations. The prolonged human childhood created by evolution and the extended period of formal education and training that society has provided for adolescents are clear responses to the degree of this difficulty. In young people, drug use interrupts and takes over this maturation process.

When young people use drugs to solve problems, they forfeit the opportunity to develop and practice adaptive responses. How does an adolescent learn to deal appropriately with the pressures to succeed in school, with the disappointment of being dumped by a boyfriend or even with the complex experience of falling in love? If she "gets high" to deal with or avoid these experiences, then she never learns responses that can build the foundation for a happy and productive life. When adults use drugs to cope with their problems, they, too, undermine the adaptive responses they might have learned, and they fail to develop the new ones that are needed to survive in our continuously changing world.

Therefore, another result of the learning that takes place during drug use is that other kinds of learning, the kinds we need throughout our lives, fail to take place or are undermined. It is true that the high school basketball star who spends all his time practicing spin moves and jump shots rather than studying is at risk of failing in college because he never learned how to study. It is also true that the high school student who abuses drugs is at risk of failing in life and becoming an addict because he never learned how to live. On top of all the other things drugs may have done, getting and using drugs just took too much time, so other activities got pushed aside.

As we explore the physiological changes that are part of addiction, such as tolerance and physical dependence, it is important to keep in mind the crucial role of *learning* in the creation of an addict. If a person repeatedly uses drugs . . . physiological changes occur gradually, but inevitably. The learning we have described . . . —conscious, explicit learning and unconscious, implicit learning, including both operant and classical conditioning—occurs in parallel. At some as yet unidentifiable point in this progression—experimentation, more regular use, tolerance, physical dependence, and psychological dependence—a controllable *desire* for drugs turns into a compelling *need* for drugs. Scientists believe that this switch takes place because of a change in the brain's reward system. Once it does occur, drug users . . . become fully addicted and lose control of their drug-taking behavior.

7

Access to and Acceptance of Drugs Contribute to Addiction

David T. Courtwright

David T. Courtwright is a professor of history at the University of North Florida. He has written Forces of Habit: Drugs and the Making of the Modern World *and* Dark Paradise: A History of Opiate Addiction in America.

If a community is accepting of drug use, higher rates of addiction will occur. Conversely, if there is a taboo against intoxication, the community will experience lower rates of addiction. Indeed, many people begin using drugs because they are fashionable; even people reluctant to experiment with drugs will be pressured to do so by their peers. Once a community has accepted the use of a drug, then use of this drug will continue through many generations.

D rugs are poisons. Psychoactive plant alkaloids evolved as a defense mechanism against herbivores. Insects and animals who eat them become dizzy and disoriented, or experience hallucinations. Yet some persist in eating intoxicating plants and fermented fruit, even though they disrupt their repertoire of survival skills. In evolutionary terms, *accidental* intoxication may be valuable: it warns an organism not to go near the plant again. *Seeking* intoxication, let alone profiting from it, is paradoxical. It seemingly defies the logic of natural selection.

David T. Courtwright, *Forces of Habit: Drugs and the Making of the Modern World.* Cambridge, MA: Harvard University Press, 2001. Copyright © 2001 by the President and Fellows of Harvard College. All rights reserved. Reproduced by permission.

Drugs Satisfy a Basic Need

One possible explanation is that the consumption of intoxicants satisfies a basic need. All people, argues [health guru] Andrew Weil, possess an innate drive to alter their normal consciousness. Children at play will whirl themselves into a vertiginous stupor; holy men and women lose themselves in meditation. The desire to vacate ego-centered consciousness is deep-seated. However, some means of achieving this end are more dangerous than others. Drugs are powerful chemical shortcuts to altered states of mind. They do not alone determine the final state, which is a product of their interaction with the user's expectations ("set") and physical and social environment ("setting"). But they are key ingredients. Anyone who uses them to satisfy the drive is trading off toxic effects for potency and rapidity of action.

> *The misery and grinding poverty . . . [of] the early modern world go far toward explaining why tobacco and other novel drugs became objects of mass consumption.*

Although Weil's postulated drive may be inborn, social circumstances have much to do with its strength. Bored, miserable creatures are more likely to seek altered consciousness than engaged, contented ones. Animals in captivity, for example, are much more likely to use intoxicants than those in the wild. And one could say that civilization itself represents a state of captivity. Humans evolved as hunter-gatherers in itinerant bands. After the Neolithic Revolution, most of them lived as peasants in crowded, oppressive, and disease-ridden societies. The misery and grinding poverty that were the lot of 90 percent of humanity in the early modern world go far toward explaining why tobacco and other novel drugs became objects of mass consumption. They were unexpected weapons against the human condition, newfound tools of escape from the mean prison of everyday existence. "There is no more profound way of understanding the course of history," [psychiatrist and researcher] Nathan Kline wrote, "than in terms of this effort to escape from one's own 'sweating self' and to experience even temporary states of euphoria or relief of discomfort regardless of the cost."

Euphoria and relief are products of a molecular accident. Only a few toxic alkaloids have molecules that, if they succeed in entering the circulatory system and passing the blood-brain barrier, mimic or influence neurotransmitters in the brain's reward and pain-control centers. Nature is parsimonious with pleasure. Euphoria-inducing neurotransmitters are ordinarily meted out frugally and for some accomplishment that enhances survival or reproduction. Drugs fool the system, temporarily increasing the level of these pleasure-inducing neurotransmitters.

How Drugs Affect the Brain

Though scientific knowledge has accumulated rapidly in the last three decades, researchers still do not know all of the ways the brain responds to different psychoactive drugs. Some, particularly alcohol, are "messy" in that they affect several neural systems. But they do appear to have at least one common denominator. They affect—directly or indirectly, strongly or weakly—the mesolimbic dopamine system, a primitive neural substrate that serves as a key pathway for pleasure and means of providing motivation for the choices we make. Drugs stimulate this system, and perhaps others not yet identified, signaling "good choice" by way of good feelings. Even a relatively nonintoxicating drug like coffee markedly elevates mood. A carefully controlled study of coffee drinking among nurses showed that those who drank two to three cups daily committed suicide only about a third as often as abstainers. It is a fascinating finding, entirely consistent with the notion of drugs as a coping tool.

> **If that supply [of external chemicals] ceases, unpleasant consequences follow.**

Before refilling your mug, however, bear in mind that the repeated use of caffeine and other drugs also alters the brain's natural chemistry in ways that are not healthful. Awash with external chemicals, the brain adjusts production of their internal equivalents or the number of receptors, becoming dependent on an outside supply. If that supply ceases, unpleasant consequences follow. Opiate withdrawal in particular triggers a cascade of symptoms: restlessness, sweating, extreme anxiety, depression, irritability, dysphoria, insomnia, fever, chills, retching and vomiting, explosive diarrhea, flu-like aches and pains. The cumulative misery has tempted many patients to suicide, as may be seen in the 1925 case history of Hermann Göring:

> Cause of illness: abuse of Morphine and Eukodal; severe withdrawal symptoms. . . . The patient holds a prominent place in the "Hitler party" in Germany, took part in the Hitler putsch, during which he was injured and hospitalized; says he escaped from there to Austria, was given morphine by the doctors at the hospital, after which he became addicted to morphine. Admitted to Aspuddens [Nursing Home], the patient manifested violent withdrawal symptoms (in spite of the nurse allowing him more morphine), during which he became threatening and so violent that he could no longer be kept there. Threatened to take his own life, wanted to "die like a man," threatened to commit hara-kiri, and so on.

That Göring, winner of the *Pour le Mérite* (the "Blue Max"), should sink to such a state, or that he should continue to use opiates intermittently for the next twenty years, nodding off in *Luftwaffe* [German air force] staff meetings, is a testament to the extraordinary hold this class of drugs can exert on the human system. "When the druggist sells me my daily box of Eukodol [*sic*] ampules he smirks like I had picked up the bait to a trap," [author] William S. Burroughs wrote [poet] Allen Ginsberg from Tangier in 1954. "Allen, I never had a habit like this before. Shooting every *two hours*. Maybe it is the Eukodol, which is semisynthetic. Trust the Germans to concoct some really evil shit."

> **"** *The notion of reversal of effects helps to explain the paradox of why people persist in manifestly unhealthful behavior.* **"**

Physical and psychological withdrawal symptoms can follow the regular use of any of the principal psychoactive commodities, including the less potent ones like caffeinated beverages. In 1989 doctors at London's Hammersmith Hospital discovered that the headaches commonly experienced by postoperative patients had nothing to do with anesthesia. They were a consequence of abstaining from caffeinated beverages before and during surgery. Depression, fatigue, and lethargy are other common symptoms. Though withdrawal is not synonymous with addiction, researchers have nevertheless found unequivocal evidence of a "caffeine dependence syndrome." This refers to patients who go to extremes to obtain caffeinated drinks, use them in dangerous or inappropriate situations, and continue drinking them despite adverse health consequences and warnings by their physicians. [French novelist] Honoré de Balzac, whose stubborn devotion to coffee hastened his death from heart disease, is the historical prototype.

> *Personal values determine whether people use, persist in using, become addicted to, and quit using drugs.*

The notion of *reversal of effects* helps to explain the paradox of why people persist in manifestly unhealthful behavior. They have, as Burroughs put it, walked into a trap baited with pleasure. Having begun using the drug to feel good, they dare not stop for fear of feeling bad. If addiction is the hijacking of the body's natural reinforcement mechanisms, withdrawal is the gun held to the head. Even addicts who detoxify completely—a process that can extend over many months for a drug like cocaine—are not the same afterwards. The brain remembers the chemical shortcuts to pleasure. Environmental cues such as a familiar tavern sign can trigger powerful cravings. Addiction is a chronic, relapsing brain disease.

How Exposure Affects Addiction

The last sentence takes us into fiercely contested terrain. . . . It is necessary to take a closer look at compulsive use. Is it fundamentally a problem of repeatedly exposing brain cells to drugs? Or is it a problem of individuals who happen to have the wrong genetic, psychological, social, cultural, and/or moral characteristics? This issue has enormous implications for both under-standing the history of drugs and implementing policies for their intelligent control.

At one extreme of the debate is a figure like [Swedish scientist] Nils Bejerot who views drugs as germ-like pathogens that can artificially induce destructive drives in anyone: "No disturbed personality and no underlying social problems are required for an individual to develop a drug dependence." Exposure is the crucial variable. It explains why physicians in Germany, the United States, and other countries have historically had narcotic addiction rates up to 100 times that of the general population. "We almost never find a lawyer who plays around with the stuff," [former drug czar] Harry Anslinger once remarked, "and nobody can tell me that lawyers are more moral or less inclined to get into trouble than doctors or nurses. You can't get away from it—if people lay their hands on the stuff, there are always a few who will try." Salvation lay in supply control.

> *Proximity, and hence familiarity and availability, matters.*

At the other extreme is a figure like [commentator] Stanton Peele who views addiction as a people problem, not a drug problem. Addiction has nothing to do with a drug or its chemical properties. Indeed, people can become addicted to activities like gambling or drug treatment itself. In this view, addicts are essentially inadequate or misguided personalities who return again and again to drugs (or their behavioral equivalents) for a "reassuring absorption into a consuming sensation which takes away all consciousness of life's problems." Personal values determine whether people use, persist in using, become addicted to, and quit using drugs. Cultural values in turn shape personal ones. Cultures that tolerate drunkenness and invest alcohol with the power to control behavior suffer worse alcohol problems than those that frown on drunkenness and hold the individual accountable. Hence alcoholism is more widespread in Ireland than in Italy, despite high levels of per capita consumption in both countries. Supply matters less than the personal and cultural values that modulate demand and comportment.

My own view of the matter (and that of most drug producers, distributors, and advertisers) is that both of these seemingly contradictory positions are true, though exposure is the critical precondition. Addiction following the use of any drug is the exception, not the rule. Only about a third of the young people who experiment with cigarettes, one of the most powerful addictive products known, become dependent users. Many individuals have inborn characteristics that confer immunity. The philosopher Karl Popper became so allergic to cigarette smoke that he turned into a virtual recluse. The real reason Bill Clinton didn't inhale marijuana is that he couldn't tolerate smoke in his lungs, despite repeated efforts by his friends to instruct him in this essential Oxonian art. Anyone with a persistent, violent reaction to a drug is essentially addiction-proof. Those with strong superegos and religious scruples are similarly less prone to experiment. Their opposite numbers, thrill-seeking sociopaths, are far more likely to light up. Peele has a point: individual values matter. So do collective ones. A strong taboo against consuming (as opposed to exporting) opium helped the Turks avoid a major addiction problem. LSD never became popular in Chinese cultures that equated hallucination with mental illness. The indulgent Japanese attitude toward alcohol abuse, by contrast, diminished the protective effect of the flushing genes carried by half its population.

Exposure and the History of Drug Use

Yet history furnishes equally dramatic lessons about the importance of exposure. Iranian opium production expanded rapidly in the second half of the nineteenth century. The silk industry went into decline, and opium seemed an attractive export crop for which there was rising world demand. But with time the exports fell, and large numbers of Iranians took to obliterating their miseries with home-grown opium. An estimated 2.8 million of them were addicts when Reza Shah Pahlavi's government attempted to eliminate production in the mid-1950s. The predictable result was fewer addicts, somewhere between a quarter and a half million in 1968, but more users of smuggled heroin. Heroin smuggled from neighboring countries also proved to be the bane of the Shah's puritanical successors. Though they launched a crusade against narcotics, hanging dealers by the score, they could not stanch the flow of heroin from Afghanistan and Pakistan. Nor could they ease the severe unemployment that tempted Iranians to engage in drug use and trafficking.

That Cubans once smoked 30 percent of all cigars made in Cuba, that Asian communities which grow and sell opium have consistently higher addiction rates than those which do not, that African transshipment points like Ghana or Nigeria have developed serious heroin and cocaine problems, that Kentuckians suffer exceptionally high rates of lung cancer—all of this strongly suggests that proximity, and hence familiarity and availability, matters. But how much? In 1973 Philip Baridon published the results of a unique global study in which he compiled officially reported addiction rates for 33 countries. He then compared these rates to twelve independent social, economic, and geographic variables (for example, urbanization, per capita income, proximity to opium- and coca-producing areas) in a multiple-regression analysis (a statistical technique for estimating relative causal weights). Proximity alone explained 45 percent of the variance, far more than any other variable. "The most fundamental fact about drug abuse is frequently overlooked in the welter of complicated psycho-social explanations," Baridon concluded. "If the drug is not available, there will be no abuse of it."

> **❝** So integral did cigarettes become to twentieth-century social life that some people took to describing them as surrogate persons. **❞**

This is why drug history is replete with giveaway promotions: bottles of Vin Mariani, cigarettes during rush week, smokeless tobacco at drag races, and surplus Brazilian coffee shipped gratis to Japan. The providers of the celebrated "free lunch" that accompanied the not-so-free beer in American workingmen's saloons a century ago played a clever variation on this theme. One Chicago salesman confided to a fellow worker that "he had had to swear off the free lunch when he realized he was beginning to go to saloons more for the beer than for the food." The idea behind all such schemes is to expose potential lifelong customers, particularly young ones whose consumption habits are still plastic. Young, single, undersocialized urban males who lack genetic or cultural protections and who are already using other drugs are on the A-list of susceptibility. They are most likely to experiment with and eventually become addicted to novel drugs, although, as Bejerot insisted, they are not the only types of people who become compulsive users. Given enough time and exposure, millions of others may join them. In 1915 American cigarette smokers were mostly confined to pool halls and street corners. In 1955 two-thirds of all American men between 25 and 64 smoked regularly, the vast majority of them cigarettes. . . .

Drugs and Fashion

Drugs are also fashion-proof—a counterintuitive claim that needs some elaboration. Particular brands and modes of administration come and go: 101-millimeter cigarettes, cocaine free-base kits. But, once established, a drug will typically persist in some form across many generations. Drugs have legs. They have outlasted beaver hats and hoop skirts and other once-fashionable items long since relegated to museums. Historically, fashion has moved from the upper to the lower classes in a "chase and flight" pattern. Social inferiors, anxious for marks of status, copy novel modes of upper-class dress, decoration, and behavior. The elites, vigilant in defense of social distinctions, then drop the vulgarized styles and practices. They move on to something else, which is copied in turn. Thus fashion constantly changes, or, as Georg Simmel wrote in a famous essay, "as it spreads it gradually goes to its doom."

> *Drugs and their affiliated pleasures are self-advertising, especially within deviant hedonic subcultures.*

Coffee, tea, and chocolate were fashionable upper-class drinks in Europe before they passed into more general use. Why weren't the silver pots retired to the townhouse attics when commoners began imbibing? One answer is that these drinks (and perhaps the sugar so liberally spooned into them) possessed properties of physical reinforcement and habituation that the latest styles in dresses did not. British aristocrats might hold their gilt-rimmed cups in dainty fashion, signaling their status with refined manners, but they were not about to give up their beloved tea. . . .

The appeal of drugs, in short, lies in their social utility as well as brain reward. Culture shapes drug use, but drugs also shape culture, inspiring all sorts of social practices, from ceremonial toasts to coffee breaks. After World War I, American women found the cigarette to be much more than a drug-delivery vehicle. It was a useful prop in their role as newly public persons, a protean symbol of independence, availability, friendship, or—stubbed out vigorously in an ashtray—of anger and defiance. So integral did cigarettes become to twentieth-century social life that some people took to describing them as surrogate persons. "I find that it's like a companion," said one woman, who smoked when her husband was away. "It's like being in company with somebody," said a man, describing his feeling of smoking alone in the woods while hunting.

By the mid–twentieth century, when nicotinic breath had become a romantic given, smoking served as a frequent accompaniment to lovemaking. So did alcohol, an ancient sexual facilitator whose amorous use remained widespread. "*No* is an extraordinarily complicated word when you're drunk," summed up the writer Caroline Knapp, who in her drinking days made it a point never to date an abstemious man. Alcohol, however, is more useful in the early stages of lovemaking than in its consummation. "It provokes the desire," as the porter says to Macduff [in Shakespeare's *Macbeth*], "but it takes away the performance." . . .

How Drugs Are Sold

While modern advertising consciously reinforces these connections, at least for licit drugs, it does not usually create them, nor is it indispensable to the process. Word of mouth—the hushed advice in the tavern, the graffiti in the *pissoir*—is more ancient and fundamental. Drugs and their affiliated pleasures are self-advertising, especially within deviant hedonic subcultures. Heroin, for example, first got its reputation for prolonging intercourse among young men who frequented the vice districts of northeastern U.S. cities—one reason its use spread rapidly within this group.

Word of mouth helps in another way. Some people fall in love with drugs the first time they take them. "You can never top that first rush," Jim Carroll wrote of heroin in *The Basketball Diaries*, "it's like ten orgasms." The more usual reaction, however, is distaste or outright sickness. Sometimes the sickness is mixed with pleasure, sometimes not. Bitterness, acrid smoke, and vomiting are visceral forms of sales resistance and the greatest drawbacks of drugs as products. Like Elizabeth I, who was said to have given up smoking after one trial, many dabblers never try again. They submit to the evolutionary logic of toxic alkaloids.

Yet others persist. Peer advice and pressure are crucial to their efforts. Don't worry, everybody gets sick the first time. It's no disgrace. You'll get the good out of it next time. And if you can't get the hang of it, well, too bad. Early twentieth-century Russian workers ridiculed the rare comrade who refused to drink as a *krasnaia devitsa* (red maiden), *mokraia kuritsa* (wet hen), or *baba* (peasant woman)—all feminine forms. Real men could handle liquor. And tobacco. "They can't believe I don't smoke," [author] Frank McCourt wrote of his youthful Irish companions. "They want to know if there's something wrong with me, the bad eyes or consumption maybe. How can you go with a girl if you don't smoke?" "You couldn't get anywhere, in the high-school society of the late forties, without smoking," agreed his American contemporary, [writer] John Updike. Though he found his first drags disagreeable, Updike gamely stuck with it, and went on smoking for more than 30 years.

8

National Trauma May Not Lead to Addiction

M.W. Bud Perrine et al.

M.W. Bud Perrine, Kerstin E.E. Schroder, Renée Forester, Pamela McGonagle-Moulton, and Frances Huessy work for the Vermont Alcohol Research Center.

The terrorist attacks on September 11, 2001, had a profound effect on Americans. In a study on drinkers in Vermont, about three hundred miles away from the epicenter, it was found that this act of terrorism led to emotional distress, but not to increased alcohol use or abuse. While people drank more on September 11, they did not drink more on days following the attacks. This study suggests that national traumas such as terrorist attacks do not lead to increased rates of addiction.

S eptember 11, 2001, is another date that will live in infamy, to paraphrase President Franklin D. Roosevelt (referring to the attack on Pearl Harbor, December 7, 1941). In the days following September 11, the terrorist attacks on the World Trade Center and the Pentagon, and the site of the airplane crash in Pennsylvania, were shown repeatedly on television to millions of viewers in the United States and around the world. How did the terrorist attacks affect the people living in the United States? The present article examines the effects of September 11 on alcohol consumption and self-rated levels of stress, anger and sadness in a sample of light, medium and heavy drinkers

M.W. Bud Perrine, Kerstin E.E. Schroder, Renée Forester, Pamela McGonagle-Moulton, and Frances Huessy, "The Impact of the September 11, 2001, Terrorist Attacks on Alcohol Consumption and Distress: Reactions to a National Trauma 300 Miles from Ground Zero," *Journal of Studies on Alcohol*, vol. 65, January 2004, pp. 5–15. Copyright © 2004 by Alcohol Research Documentation, Inc., Rutgers University Center of Alcohol Studies, Piscataway, NJ 08854. Reproduced by permission.

in Vermont hundreds of miles away from New York City, Washington, D.C., and Pennsylvania. . . .

Psychological Aims and Effects of Terrorism

To date, little research has been conducted on the effects of terrorism on indirect targets of an attacked society. Studies on terrorism usually focus on immediate victims, survivors, direct witnesses or people living in locations close to an attack to evaluate personal trauma, mental health and health behaviors. As a consequence of this focus on victimization and trauma, these studies have much in common with research on natural or technological disaster, mass violence or personal injury and loss.

Terrorism, however, is defined by specific features that call for research on the vicarious experience of terrorism. In contrast to other kinds of disaster, terrorism is defined [by the Terrorism Research Center] as "the calculated use of violence or the threat of violence to inculcate fear . . . intended to coerce or to intimidate governments or societies in the pursuit of goals that are generally political, religious, or ideological".

> *In both [men and women] marked increases were found for all three measures of emotional distress.*

Terrorist acts are designed to traumatize and do, in fact, correspond to current knowledge on trauma induction. In this context, the September 11 attacks appear as the prototype of calculated, organized aggression that was most likely to cause a severe, sustained and widespread national trauma in the U.S. population. . . .

Drinking on and After September 11

Two sets of preliminary analyses were performed. First, men and women were compared on the demographic variables, including age, education, income, employment, highest grade in school, ethnicity, marital status, number of children, number of people living in the household and current as well as lifetime symptoms and abuse. No significant differences were found between men and women in any of the demographic variables. Second, gender differences were examined in alcohol consumption and mood before, during and following September 11. Gender differences preceding Tuesday, September 11, were weak and limited to alcohol consumption only. During baseline, on average, men had 4.7 drinks and women 3.2 drinks per day. . . . Similarly, when we look at average daily consumption on Tuesdays only, men drank significantly more (3.8 drinks) than women (2.5 drinks). . . . In contrast, no differences emerged between men and women in the number of drinks consumed on September 11. However, in both samples marked increases were found for all three measures of emotional distress on September 11, with women scoring significantly higher than men. In the 110 days following September 11 (09/12/01 to 12/30/01), emotional distress approached baseline levels. . . .

> *Vicarious experience of a national trauma does not necessarily affect drinking behavior in a population remote from the events.*

With the average alcohol consumption on the previous 52 Tuesdays [before September 11] for comparison, descriptive analyses revealed that men consumed 14% more alcohol (about 0.5 drinks) and women consumed 34% more alcohol (0.8 drinks) on Tuesday, September 11, 2001. Compared with the 365 days preceding September 11, no increases in alcohol consumption appeared on or following September 11 for either men or women. Moreover, alcohol consumption did not appear as being out of control. . . .

The Effects of National Trauma

The present post–September 11 study examined the effects of a national trauma on contemporaneous self-reports of alcohol consumption and emotional distress. Daily self-reports, collected for a total of 476 days between September 11, 2000, and December 30, 2001, were analyzed by means of statistical process control. In regard to the study hypotheses, the following conclusions can be drawn.

No remarkable changes in alcohol consumption occurred in

response to the terrorist attacks. Increases in alcohol consumption were limited to the female sample [and] emerged on the day of September 11 only. . . . These results, based on near-contemporaneous reports, suggest that vicarious experience of a national trauma does not necessarily affect drinking behavior in a population remote from the events, which contrasts with retrospective reports of increased alcohol consumption close to the epicenter of a terrorist attack.

Immediate emotional reactions to the September 11 attacks were marked among both men and women. Time periods until return to baseline levels varied substantially according to gender, with a range from 4 to 70 days. Sadness was the predominant and most persistent reaction among both genders, remaining elevated for 36 days among men and 70 days among women. The amount of time needed to return to baseline levels of emotional distress may mirror the continued attention paid to the coverage of the events in the media in the weeks and months following the attacks. In sum, the results indicate that vicarious experience of terrorism elicits strong emotional responses among members of a victimized society, even in areas remote from the epicenters. The results are congruent with retrospective findings of PTSD [post traumatic stress disorder] symptoms following the September 11 attacks in a representative sample of the U.S. population. . . .

The lack of correspondence between changes in emotional distress and alcohol consumption in the present study requires explanation. It contradicts retrospective reports of increased alcohol consumption in populations close to the epicenter and suggests that, under conditions of vicarious experience of terror, emotional distress may fail to produce any remarkable effects on alcohol consumption. The present results contradict a potential explanation that lack of emotional response weakened potential effects of September 11 on alcohol consumption. Vicarious experience of trauma, however, may lack sufficient personal involvement to establish a causal link between emotional distress and drinking. . . . Thus, although the participants in the present study reported strong emotional reactions, the experience of personal threat or loss was absent. It appears that under these circumstances an increase in alcohol consumption may not occur as a response to emotional distress.

Organizations to Contact

The editors have compiled the following list of organizations concerned with the issues debated in this book. The descriptions are derived from materials provided by the organizations. All have publications or information available for interested readers. The list was compiled on the date of publication of the present volume; names, addresses, phone and fax numbers, and e-mail addresses may change. Be aware that many organizations take several weeks or longer to respond to inquiries, so allow as much time as possible.

Addiction Science Research and Education Center at the University of Texas (ASREC)
1 University Station A1915, PHR 5.224, Austin, TX 78712-0125
(512) 471-5192 • fax: (512) 475-6088
Web site: www.utexas.edu

ASREC is a group of scientists whose mission is to communicate the latest findings in addiction science to the public, in terms that make the message easy to understand. It offers free scientifically based information on drug topics.

Al-Anon Family Group Headquarters
1600 Corporate Landing Pkwy., Virginia Beach, VA 23454-5617
(757) 563-1600 • fax: (757) 563-1635
e-mail: wso@al-anon.org • Web site: http://al-anon.alateen.org

For over fifty years, Al-Anon (which includes Alateen for younger members) has been offering hope and help to families and friends of alcoholics. Members share their experiences to help each other. Al-Anon Family Group Headquarters publishes books, pamphlets, service materials, and a monthly magazine, the *Forum*. Most Al-Anon and Alateen meetings offer complimentary literature to newcomers, and offer books and pamphlets for sale.

Alcoholics Anonymous (AA)
Grand Central Station, PO Box 459, New York, NY 10163
(212) 870-3400 • fax: (212) 870-3003
Web site: www.aa.org

Alcoholics Anonymous is a fellowship of men and women who share their experience, strength, and hope with each other so that they can solve their common problem and help others to recover from alcoholism. It publishes the *Grapevine*, a monthly newsletter that shares news from the central office and personal stories of addiction and recovery.

Canadian Centre on Substance Abuse (CCSA)
75 Albert St., Suite 300, Ottawa, ON K1P 5E7 Canada
(613) 235-4048 ext. 222 • fax: (613) 235-8108
e-mail: info@ccsa.ca • Web site: www.ccsa.ca

The CCSA is Canada's national addictions agency. Its mission is to provide objective, evidence-based information and advice that will help reduce the health, social, and economic harm associated with substance abuse and addictions. It publishes the newsletter *Action News* as well as reports and research papers.

Canadian Foundation for Drug Policy (CFDP)
10 MacDonald St., Ottawa, ON K2P 1H6 Canada
(613) 236-1027 • fax: (613) 238-2891
e-mail: eoscapel@fox.nstn.ca • Web site: www.cfdp.ca

The CFDP is a nonprofit organization founded in 1993 by several of Canada's leading specialists in drug policy. It advocates reform of Canada's drug laws to make them more effective and humane. Its Web site offers educational materials and updates on its activities.

Drug Enforcement Administration (DEA)
Mailstop: AXS, 24101 Jefferson Davis Hwy., Alexandria, VA 22301
(202) 307-1000
Web site: www.usdoj.gov/dea

The DEA enforces the controlled substances laws and regulations of the United States. It focuses on stopping the trafficking and sale of narcotics both domestically and internationally. It publishes materials on the effects of the use and distribution of narcotics on communities.

Drug Policy Alliance
925 Fifteenth St. NW, 2nd Fl., Washington, DC 20005
(202) 216-0035 • fax: (202) 216-0803
e-mail: dc@drugpolicy.org • Web site: www.dpf.org

The Drug Policy Alliance aims to advance those policies and attitudes that best reduce the harms of both drug misuse and drug prohibition. It supports the legalization of marijuana for medical purposes, making methadone maintenance and other effective drug treatment more accessible and available, and spending more government funds on public health and education. It offers information on the experiences of other countries in policies based on harm reduction as well as updates on current legislation in the United States.

DrugSense
14252 Culver Dr., #328, Irvine, CA 92604-0326
(800) 266-5759
e-mail: info@drugsense.org • Web site: www.drugsense.org

DrugsSense is an international network of activists that provides information on the damage caused to the United States and other countries by the "War on Drugs." It provides technical support for organizations interested in reforming drug policy. It maintains a database of current news and opinion articles.

Hazelden Institute
PO Box 176, Center City, MN 55012-0176
(800) 328-9000 • fax: (651) 213-4590
e-mail: info@hazelden.org • Web site: www.hazelden.org

Hazelden helps build recovery in the lives of individuals, families, and communities affected by alcoholism, drug dependency, and related diseases. It provides residential and outpatient treatment for adults and teenagers as well as programs for their families. Its Web site lists online resources for those who are struggling, or know someone who is struggling, with addiction.

Narcotics Anonymous (NA)
PO Box 9999, Van Nuys, CA 91409
(818) 773-9999 • fax: (818) 700-0700
e-mail: fsmail@na.org • Web site: www.na.org

NA grew out of AA and follows the same Twelve Steps. It is a nonprofit society of men and women for whom drugs have become a major problem. It offers weekly meetings to those looking to end their addiction to drugs. NA publishes pamphlets and other materials on its principles and goals.

National Center on Addiction and Substance Abuse at Columbia University (CASA)
633 Third Ave., 19th Fl., New York, NY 10017-6706
(212) 841-5200 • fax: (212) 956-8020
Web site: www.casa.org

CASA brings together professionals from the fields of substance abuse and addiction, communications, criminology, education, epidemiology, government, journalism, law, psychology, public administration, public health, public policy, social work, sociology, and statistics. It works to curb drug abuse by informing Americans of the economic and social costs of substance abuse and its impact on their lives, and assessing what works in prevention, treatment, and law enforcement. CASA's Web site features information on its activities in the community as well as reports on its research.

National Clearinghouse for Alcohol and Drug Information
PO Box 2345, Rockville, MD 20847-2345
(800) 729-6686 • fax: (301) 468-4633
Web site: www.health.org

The National Clearinghouse for Alcohol and Drug Information offers information from the U.S. Department of Health and Human Services and the Substance Abuse and Mental Health Services Administration on community drug prevention programs and the latest research on drug and alcohol addiction.

National Council on Alcoholism and Drug Dependence, Inc. (NCADD)
20 Exchange Pl., Suite 2902, New York, NY 10005
(212) 269-7797 • fax: (212) 269-7510
e-mail: national@ncadd.org • Web site: www.ncadd.org

NCADD is dedicated to teaching the public that alcoholism is a preventable and treatable disease, not a moral failing. It promotes Alcohol Awareness Month in April, successfully campaigned to place warning labels on all alcoholic beverage containers, and maintains a Registry of Addiction Recovery (ROAR), a volunteer program that encourages Americans all over the country to speak openly about their experiences with addiction. Information on its programs both nationally and locally is available at its Web site.

National Institute on Alcohol Abuse and Alcoholism (NIAAA)
5635 Fishers Ln., MSC 9304, Bethesda, MD 20892-9304
(301) 496-4000
e-mail: niaaaweb-r@exchange.nih.gov • Web site: www.niaaa.nih.gov

The NIAAA conducts and supports research in a wide range of scientific areas including genetics, neuroscience, epidemiology, health risks and benefits of alcohol consumption, prevention, and treatment. It seeks to remove the stigma associated with alcoholism. It also works to develop effective prevention and treatments that address the chronic relapsing nature of alcoholism, and improve the acceptance of, and access to, quality care. It publishes the quarterly journal *Alcohol Health & Research World.*

National Institute on Drug Abuse (NIDA)
5600 Fishers Ln., Rockville, MD 20857
(301) 443-1124
e-mail: Information@lists.nida.nih.gov
Web site: www.nida.nih.gov

NIDA conducts research on how drugs affect the brain and human behavior. It works with other organizations to use this research to improve addiction prevention and treatment. Its Web site offers educational resources for students and health care professionals.

National Organization for the Reform of Marijuana Laws (NORML)
1600 K St. NW, Suite 501, Washington, DC 20006-2832
(202) 483-5500 • fax: (202) 483-0057
e-mail: norml@norml.org • Web site: http://norml.org

NORML provides a voice in the public policy debate for those Americans who oppose marijuana prohibition and favor an end to the practice of arresting marijuana smokers. It lobbies state and federal legislators, fights to reform state and federal marijuana laws, and hosts an annual conference. It publishes a newsletter and other information on its Web site.

Office of National Drug Control Policy (ONDCP)
Drug Policy Information Clearinghouse, PO Box 6000, Rockville, MD 20849-6000
(800) 666-3332 • fax: (301) 519-5212
e-mail: ondcp@ncjrs.org • Web site: http://whitehousedrugpolicy.gov

The principal purpose of ONDCP is to establish policies, priorities, and objectives for the nation's drug control program. The goals of the program are to reduce illicit drug use, manufacturing, and trafficking, drug-related crime and violence, and drug-related health consequences. Its

Web site covers current drug legislation, media campaigns to prevent drug use, and current research on the effects of illicit drugs.

Partnership for a Drug-Free America (PDFA)
405 Lexington Ave., Suite 160, New York, NY 10174
(212) 922-1560 • fax: (212) 922-1570
e-mail: webmail@drugfree.org • Web site: www.drugfreeamerica.org

The PDFA is a nonprofit coalition of professionals from the communications industry. Through its national drug-education advertising campaign and other forms of media communication, the PDFA seeks to help kids and teens reject substance abuse by influencing attitudes through persuasive information. Its Web site offers stories of drug abuse, information on the effects of illicit drugs, and advice for talking to friends about their drug problems.

Bibliography

Books

Anna Alexander and Mark S. Roberts	*High Culture: Reflections on Addiction and Modernity.* Albany: State University of New York Press, 2002.
Floyd E. Bloom, M. Flint Beal, and David J. Kupfer, eds.	*The Dana Guide to Brain Health.* New York: Dana, 2003.
Brian Castellani	*Pathological Gambling: The Making of a Medical Problem.* Albany: State University of New York Press, 2000.
David T. Courtwright	*Forces of Habit: Drugs and the Making of the Modern World.* Cambridge, MA: Harvard University Press, 2001.
Richard Davenport-Hines	*The Pursuit of Oblivion: A Global History of Narcotics.* New York: Norton, 2002.
Tian Dayton	*Trauma and Addiction.* Deerfield Beach, FL: Health Communication, 2000.
Carlo C. DiClemente	*Addiction and Change: How Addictions Develop and Addicted People Recover.* New York: Guilford, 2003.
Lance M. Dodes	*The Heart of Addiction.* New York: HarperCollins, 2002.
David P. Friedman and Sue Rusche	*False Messengers: How Addictive Drugs Change the Brain.* Amsterdam, The Netherlands: Harwood Academic, 1999.
Darryl S. Inaba and William E. Cohen	*Uppers, Downers, All Arounders: The Physical and Mental Effects of Psychoactive Drugs.* Ashland, OR: CNS, 2000.
Robert M. Julien	*A Primer of Drug Action: A Concise, Nontechnical Guide to the Actions, Uses, and Side Effects of Psychoactive Drugs.* New York: Holt, 2001.
Cynthia Kuhn	*Buzzed: The Straight Facts About the Most Used and Abused Drugs from Alcohol to Ecstasy.* New York: W.W. Norton, 2003.
Michelle Lee	*Fashion Victim.* New York: Broadway, 2003.
Jane Lilianfeld and Jeffrey Oxford	*The Languages of Addiction.* New York: Palgrave Macmillan, 1999.
Meredith Maran	*Dirty: A Search for Answers Inside America's Drug Epidemic.* San Francisco: HarperSanFrancisco, 2003.

Richard Lawrence Miller	*The Encyclopedia of Addictive Drugs.* Westport, CT: Greenwood, 2002.
David F. Musto	*Drugs in America: A Documentary History.* New York: New York University Press, 2002.
Lonny Shavelson	*Hooked: Five Addicts Challenge Our Misguided Drug Rehab System.* New York: New Press, 2002.
Barbara Strauch	*The Primal Teen.* New York: Doubleday, 2003.
Jacob Sullum	*Saying Yes: In Defense of Drug Use.* New York: J.P. Tarcher/Putnam, 2003.

Periodicals

Amitabh Avasthi	"Addicted Rats Signal Hope for Humans," *New Scientist*, August 12, 2004.
Laura Berman	"What Makes a Woman a Sex Addict?" *Chicago Sun-Times*, September 6, 2004.
Shaoni Bhattacharya	"Alcoholic Blackouts May Lead to Heavier Drinking," *New Scientist*, April 14, 2003.
Shaoni Bhattacharya	"Genes Linked to High-Risk Personalities," *New Scientist*, June 17, 2003.
Bruce Bower	"Certain Mental Ills May Be Tied to Violence," *Science News*, October 28, 2000.
Bruce Bower	"Drunk Drivers Tow Mental Load," *Science News*, October 13, 2001.
Fox Butterfield	"Across Rural America, Drug Casts a Grim Shadow," *New York Times*, January 4, 2004.
Kate Figes	"At 15, I Settled for Casual Sex," *Daily Telegraph*, June 19, 2004.
Sarah Graham	"Taste Tests Could Help Identify Risk of Alcoholism," *Scientific American*, June 2003.
Laura Helmuth	"Beyond the Pleasure Principle," *Science News*, November 2, 2001.
David Hench	"Maine Tops Most States in Painkiller Use; State Officials Say the High Rate of Use Explains a Growing Problem with Prescription Drug Abuse," *Portland Press Herald*, April 5, 2004.
Constance Holden	"Behavioral Addictions: Do They Exist?" *Science News*, November 2, 2001.
Sally Lehrman	"Sobering Shift," *Scientific American*, April 2004.
William M. London	"How Addictive Is Cigarette Smoking?" *Priorities for Health*, July 1, 2000.

Cameron McWhirter and Jill Young Miller	"Meth Stalks Rural Georgia: Cheap, Easily Manufactured Stimulant Is Countryside's Fastest-Growing Drug Problem, and Abuse Can Be Deadly," *Atlanta Journal-Constitution*, June 6, 2004.
Elizabeth Mehren	"Hooks of 'Hillbilly Heroin'; Abuse of Prescription Painkiller OxyContin Ravages Poor Areas in the East," *Los Angeles Times*, October 4, 2001.
Kendall Morgan	"More than a Kick," *Science News*, March 22, 2003.
Eric J. Nestler	"Total Recall—the Memory of Addiction," *Science News*, June 22, 2001.
Eric J. Nestler and Robert C. Malenka	"The Addicted Brain," *Scientific American*, March 2004.
Jessa Netting	"Memory May Draw Addicts Back to Cocaine," *Science News*, May 12, 2001.
Office of National Drug Control Policy	"Substance Use in Popular Movies and Music," April 1999. www.mediacampaign.org.
Office of National Drug Control Policy	"Substance Use in Popular Music Videos," June 2002. www.mediacampaign.org.
Office of National Drug Control Policy	"Substance Use in Popular Prime Time Television," January 2000. www.mediacampaign.org.
John O'Neil	"Tired Toddlers, Troubled Teens," *New York Times*, April 20, 2004.
Mary Pemberton	"Alaska Struggles with Its High Rate of Suicide; Guns, Isolation, Poverty, Drug Abuse Lead State Residents to Despair," *Oakland Tribune*, December 31, 2003.
Tabitha M. Powledge	"Beating Abuse," *Scientific American*, January 2002.
Janet Raloff	"Could Nicotine Patch Fight Depression?" *Science News*, May 11, 2002.
James Randerson	"Low Rank Monkeys More Prone to Cocaine Addiction," *New Scientist*, January 20, 2002.
Irene Sege	"'I Got Caught Up in the Moment,'" *Boston Globe*, March 24, 2004.
Nathan Seppa	"Nicotine Metabolism Shows Ethnic Bias," *Science News*, January 19, 2002.
Rebecca Skloot	"Who's an Addict?" *Popular Science*, April 2002.
John Travis	"Mutant Mice Resist Morphine's Appeal," *Science News*, November 23, 2002.
Gaia Vince	"Common Gene Mutation Linked to Drug Addiction," *New Scientist*, June 10, 2002.
Claudia Voyles	"Pain and Addiction," *Guidepoints: Acupuncture in Recovery*, May 2003.

David Wahlberg   "Stronger Pot Propels Addiction Rate Higher," *Atlanta Journal-Constitution*, May 5, 2004.

Emma Young   "Gene Linked to Stress-Related Drinking," *New Scientist*, May 2, 2002.

Emma Young   "Mothers Neglect Changes Infants' Brain Development," *New Scientist*, November 15, 2001.

Index